# LEARN FRENCH GRAMMAR WORKBOOK FOR ADULT BEGINNERS

## Speak French in Just 30 Days

# CONTENTS

# DISCLAIMER NOTICE:

# INTRODUCTION

French is a fascinating language; it's the source of famous literature, legendary poems, and screenplays. It's the language artists use to convey their visions of the world. Despite being one of the most complex languages to learn, it's also one of the most in-demand.

One could argue that learning French is only for its beauty, but the truth is, it's one of the most useful languages to learn. With over 300 million people speaking it, you're bound to need it. Maybe that's the main reason you've picked up this book. However, to be honest, there are infinite reasons to get into this marvellous language. Whether it's after watching a documentary about Paris, arguably the best tourist city ever, or before embarking on a trip to a French-speaking African country, or maybe even out of admiration for one of the famous French football players. Reasons may differ, but you're always right to get started with this language.

There's a chance you've been told to give up on it, that it's too hard, or that the grammar doesn't make any sense. Maybe the person who told you that believes what they said, but chances are they never got the chance to read this book!

This workbook is the result of many years of research. With fifteen highly informative and beginner-friendly exercises, you're guaranteed to grasp the basics of French grammar in no time. You'll need to concentrate, but you won't get bored. Each lesson and exercise is specially tailored to ensure that you stay engaged as you learn. As you progress through these lessons, you'll learn essential vocabulary and grammar rules that prepare you to speak French in the real world.

Now, let's start this life-changing voyage into the French language together! Let's go!

One final thing before you start: Find your bonus content at the end of chapter 2, right before chapter 3 begins. You can go check it out right now. Enjoy!

Speak Abroad
Academy

CHAPTER 1:

# PRONOUNS AND GREETINGS
## *GOOD MORNING AND GOODBYE, FROM ME TO YOU*

First things first! The first step to learning any language always begins with subject pronouns. In English, these are words like 'I', 'you', and 'they'. They indicate who exactly we're talking about and they're essential for everyday conversation! Without them, it would be impossible to describe ourselves, other people, and how events have affected us. They're some of the most basic building blocks of any language.

So let's take a look at what subject pronouns are in French!

## 1.1 Subject Pronouns

| English | French | Pronunciation |
|---|---|---|
| I | **je** | *[jə]* |
| you *(inf., sing.)* | **tu** | *[tu]* |
| you *(form., sing.)* | **vous** | *[voo]* |
| he | **il** | *[eel]* |
| she | **elle** | *[ehl]* |
| we *(m.)*<br>we *(f.)* | **nous** | *[noo]* |
| you *(form. and inf., pl.)* | **vous** | *[voo]* |
| they *(m.)* | **ils** | *[eel]* |
| they *(f.)* | **elles** | *[ehl]* |

You'll notice that, in French, there are a lot more subject pronouns than in English! Aside from *who* they reference, they're also split up based on:

⮑ formality of the situation;

⮑ genders of the people you're talking about;

⮑ quantity of subjects, i.e. whether you're just talking about one person or more.

Unlike in English, there are different French pronouns for 'you' and 'they' depending on how many people you're talking to or talking about.

## Formal vs. Informal Pronouns

Earlier, we briefly touched on how different pronouns are used based on the formality of a situation. For example, if you were speaking directly to one person ('you'), you'd use the word **tu** in an informal situation and **vous** in a formal situation. But what exactly constitutes an informal or formal situation?

You'd use the formal word **vous** in interactions with people like:

- your boss;
- a stranger or new acquaintance (unless you want to be casual straight away);
- a salesperson;
- the cashier at the bank.

You'd use the informal pronoun tu with:

- your friends;
- your family;
- children and animals;
- people you intend to insult;
- other young people (if you're young, too).

**What if you're not sure whether to use tu or vous?**

Situations may arise where you're not sure whether to go with the informal or formal pronoun. In this case, be safe and go with the formal **vous** at first. It's much better to be overly polite than to risk coming across as rude or overly casual. In doubt, the best way is to simply ask the other person if they prefer to be called with « tu » or « vous ».

> The masculine plural form **ils** refers to a group of males or to a group that includes both males and females. The feminine plural form **elles** only refers to a group of females. In other words, the default word for 'they' is **ils**, unless you're referring to a group of people that's entirely female.

Speak Abroad
Academy

> **Interesting fact:** In French, there is no neutral subject pronoun **because there is no neutral gender. Everything, from people and objects to abstract constructs, is either masculine or feminine.** You use il and **elle** for everything. I know, it would be like calling a shoe or a potato 'he' and 'she'. Quirky, right?

Now that we've built a preliminary foundation with the use of formal and informal pronouns, it's time for a little practice to really solidify that knowledge! Are you ready?

***Note on Abbreviations: masculine (m.); feminine (f.); informal (inf.); formal (form.); singular (sing.); plural (pl.)*

## Practice 1.1 Pronouns

### A. Translate the following pronouns:

1. We (f.): _____
2. I: _____
3. They (f.): _____
4. They (m.): _____
5. You (inf.): _____
6. You (form.): _____
7. We: _____
8. They (co-ed.): _____

### B. Write the correct subject pronoun.

1. _____ vais chez toi. (*I'm going to your house.*)
2. _____ sommes tes amis. (*We* — (m.) — *are your friends.*)
3. _____ êtes les meilleurs. (*You* — (m. inf. pl.) — *are the best.*)
4. _____ êtes des hommes. (*You* — (form. inf. pl. in French-speaking-locations) — *are men.*)
5. _____ sont amis. (*They* — (m.) — *are friends.*)
6. _____ es une femme. (*You* — (sing. inf.) — *are a woman.*)

### C. Replace the names/pronouns between brackets with an adequate pronoun:

1. {They} _____ vont manger (*will eat*) au restaurant (*at the restaurant*).
2. {You – form.} _____ êtes invité au mariage (*are invited to the wedding*).

3. _____ {Elise and you/inf.}, voulez-vous aller au mariage (*want to go to the wedding)?*

4. {Thomas and I} _____ avons une surprise (*have a surprise*).

5. {Samuel} _____ vit au Québec (*lives in Quebec*).

6. {Julie} _____ vit en France (*lives in France*).

**D. What would you say with each of the following, tu or vous?**

1. Your grandmother _____
2. A coworker _____
3. A flight attendant _____
4. Your boss _____
5. A little boy _____
6. A professor _____
7. A repair person _____
8. Your cousin _____
9. Your best friend _____
10. Your father-in-law _____

**E. Say which pronoun you would use according to the situation: tu or vous**

1. You tell your close friend: «_____ sais très bien cuisiner. » (*You're very good at cooking*)

2. You ask the waiter at a restaurant when your table will be ready. He answers: « _____ êtes les suivants. » (*You're next*)

3. You ask your siblings if they want to come with you to the park: « _____ voulez venir avec moi ? » (*Do you want to come?*)

4. You tell your friends that they're your best friends: « _____ êtes mes meilleurs amis » (*You are my best friends*)

5. You compliment your doctor: « _____ êtes si intelligent. » (*You're so intelligent*)

# 1.2   Greetings and Polite Expressions

As we mentioned earlier, your word choices will vary depending on the formality of the situation. This applies not only to pronouns but also to longer exchanges, like greetings. In English, formality and informality matter too! For example, you probably wouldn't enter a formal meeting with your boss and say, 'Hey, what's up?'

In French, it's no different. You'll have different greetings for different types of situations. The words might essentially mean the same thing, but the choices convey whether you're familiar or unfamiliar with the person or people you're addressing.

Speak Abroad
Academy

## Informal Greeting

Consider the following informal greeting between Amélie and François, two young housemates who go to the same college. Since they're both peers, they'll use informal language with each other, even if they're not that close.

Amélie :       Salut, François.
               *(Hi, François.)*

François :     Salut Amélie. Ça va ?
               *(Hi, Amélie. How's it going?)*

Amélie :       Bien. Et toi ?
               *(Good. And you?)*

François:      Ça va bien ! À tout à l'heure.
               *(Very good! See you later.)*

Amélie :       Bye.
               *(Bye.)*

## Formal Greeting

Now, let's look at a formal greeting between Monsieur Delort and Madame Morgane. Monsieur Delort is a security guard at Madame Morgane's apartment building. Even though they're both middle-aged, they would use formal language with each other, since they don't know each other well, and they aren't exactly peers.

Monsieur Delort :       Bonjour, Madame Morgane.
                        *(Good afternoon, Madame Morgane.)*

Madame Morgane :        Bonjour, Monsieur Delort. Comment allez-vous ?
                        *(Good afternoon, Monsieur Delort. How are you?)*

Monsieur Delort :       Très bien, merci. Et vous ?
                        *(Very good, thank you. And you?)*

Madame Morgane :        Très bien, merci. Au revoir.
                        *(Very good, thanks. Goodbye.)*

Monsieur Delort :       Au revoir.
                        *(Goodbye.)*

Both the informal and formal greetings essentially say the same thing, but they'll use different words in the formal exchange to express politeness. That said, some words and phrases will remain the same. You can still say **bien** or **très bien** to say *you're doing well* or *very well*, and in either situation, you can still say **au revoir** to say *goodbye*.

## Vocabulary: Basic Greetings

| English | French | Pronunciation |
|---|---|---|
| Hi | **Salut** | [sah-lu] |
| How's it going? | **Ça va ?** | [sah vah] |
| Good | **Bien** | [byahn] |
| And you? | **Et toi ?** | [ay twah] |
| Very good | **Très bien** | [tray byahn] |
| See you later | **À la prochaine** | [a la prɔʃɛn] |
| Goodbye | **Au revoir** | [oh rə-vwahr] |
| Bye | **Ciao** | [chaw] |

> **Tip: Ça va ?** and **Et toi ?** are greeting expressions used in informal situations, with people you know well, on a first-name basis.

## Vocabulary: Other Greetings

| English | French | Pronunciation |
|---|---|---|
| Good morning/Hello | **Bonjour** | [bo~-joor] |
| Good afternoon | **Bonjour** | [bo~-joor] |
| Good evening, good night | **Bonsoir** | [bo~ swahr] |
| Good night | **Bonne nuit** | [bo~ nwee] |
| Mr. | **Monsieur (M.)** | [mø-syø] |
| Mrs. | **Madame (Mme)** | [mah-dahm] |
| Miss | **Mademoiselle (Mlle)** | [mah-də-mwah-zayl] |
| How are you? | **Comment allez-vous?** | [koh-mo~ ah-lay voo] |
| And you? | **Et vous ?** | [ay voo] |
| See you soon | **À bientôt** | [ah byah-toh] |
| See you tomorrow | **À demain** | [ah də-mahn] |
| Have a good afternoon | **Bon après-midi** | [bo~ apray mee-dee] |

**Speak Abroad**
Academy

Did you notice that « Bonjour » is used at different times of the day? It's because this is the most common way to say 'Hello' in French. However, « Bonsoir » means 'Good evening' (greetings) and 'Good night' (when you leave the room). But if you wanted to wish someone good night (when you leave) or when you're going to bed, it's « Bonne nuit » = 'Sweet dreams').

> **Tip: Comment allez-vous ?** and **Et vous ?** are used to address someone with whom you have a more formal relationship, like your boss or a salesperson – or to address a group of people, of course. (with plural « vous »)

## 1.3 Language Etiquette

Next, we have the 'magic' words and phrases that will help you address others politely in everyday life. Remember to say 'please' and 'thank you' in French, just as you do in English.

| English | French | Pronunciation |
|---|---|---|
| Thanks / Thank you | **Merci** | *[mayr-see]* |
| Thanks a lot / Thank you very much | **Merci beaucoup** | *[mayr-see boh-koo]* |
| You're welcome | **De rien** | *[də ryahn]* |
| Please | **S'il te plaît** | *[seel tə play]* |
| Please (form. or to address a group) | **S'il vous plaît** | *[seel voo play]* |
| It's nothing / No problem | **Pas de problème** | *[pah də proh/blaym]* |
| Excuse me / Pardon me (to get someone's attention or to apologize to someone for something you did) | **Pardon** | *[pahr-do~]* |
| Excuse me (to get someone's attention or to apologize to someone for something you did) | **Excusez-moi** | *[ayx-ku-zay mwah]* |

## Practice 1.3 Language Etiquette

**A. Choose the most appropriate response from the list on the right to the following greetings or expressions:**

1. Merci beaucoup. _____      a) Bonsoir.
2. Bonjour. _____      b) Bien, merci, et vous ?
3. Comment allez-vous ? _____      c) De rien.
4. Ça va ? _____      d) Bonjour, comment allez-vous ?
5. Bye. _____      e) Bien, et toi ?
6. Bonsoir. _____      f) Au revoir.

**B. What might these people say to each other if they met or passed each other at the time given?**

1. Laura and Matthew at 2.00 p.m.
2. Mary and her boss at 7.00 a.m.
3. You and your friend at noon.
4. Joe and Ann at 7.00 p.m.
5. You and your Math teacher at 11 a.m.

**C. Match the situation with what you say if it happens**

1. You accidentally bump into a person on the street.      a) Excusez-moi.
2. You thank someone for helping you with your luggage.      b) Pas de problème.
3. You're trying to get the attention of a waiter.      c) Merci beaucoup.
4. Your friend is grateful that you're lending him some money.      d) S'il vous plaît.
5. An elderly woman thanks you for helping her cross the street.      e) De rien.

**D. Choose the most appropriate response to the following statements or questions**

1. Merci beaucoup.
2. Ça va ?
3. Comment allez-vous ?
4. Ciao.
5. Désolé.

a) Au revoir.
b) Pas de problème.
c) Bien, et toi ?
d) Très bien, merci.
e) De rien.

**E. Complete the following dialogue with the right greeting or phrase.**

1. YOU: Salut François, _____ [1] ?
2. François: Bien, merci, _____ [2] ?
3. YOU: Très _____ [3].
4. François: Ciao. _____ [4] demain.
5. YOU: _____ [5].

**CHAPTER 2:**

# NOUNS AND ARTICLES

*THE DOG AND THE CAT*

## 2.1 The Gender of Nouns and the Singular Definite Article

Now that we've dipped our toes into pronouns, let's navigate the captivating world of nouns in French. Nouns are the building blocks of language representing objects, places, and things.

Unlike English, all nouns in French are either masculine or feminine. This doesn't mean that objects are perceived as having literal gender differences, of course, but rather, they are just classified into different groups.

Some of these are straightforward, such as **l'homme** and **la femme,** which mean *the man* and *the woman* respectively. As you'd expect, **homme** is a masculine noun and **femme** is a feminine noun. Although they're different words, **le** and **la** both mean *'the'* – they simply apply to different genders. You would never ever say « **la homme** » or « **le femme** » as it would be grammatically incorrect.

It's easy with people, but less so with objects and places. To speak fluent French, you'll need to get used to the genders of different nouns. For example, you'll need to remember that *a book* is masculine while *a photograph* is feminine.

To make this easier, picture this: learning French is like having a conversation with objects, and they come in two fashionable outfits (masculine and feminine). Imagine strolling through a linguistic wardrobe where a book confidently sports a bow tie (m.), while a photograph gracefully dons a flowing gown (f.). So, when you're chatting *en français*, it's not just about words; it's a sartorial adventure through the gendered closets of nouns!

Therefore, it's important that the definite article (*the*) should always agree with the gender of the noun. This is a hard one for English speakers, because we only have one definite article — 'the' — and don't have to worry about the rest! With practice, you'll get the hang of it.

**Speak Abroad**
Academy

## Singular Masculine Nouns

As we mentioned earlier, the masculine singular noun uses the definite article « **le** ». This shows we are referring to just one thing, place, or object. Don't worry about plural nouns for now; we'll get to those later.

Watch out, though. If the noun that follows starts with a vowel or a silent 'H', you need to use « **l'** » instead. So, don't say « le homme », but « l'homme ».

| English | French | Pronunciation |
|---|---|---|
| The man | **l'homme** | [lohm] |
| The friend (male) | **l'ami** | [lah-mee] |
| The boy | **le garçon** | [lə gahr/soh~] |
| The son | **le fils** | [lə fees] |
| The brother | **le frère** | [lə frayr] |
| The grandfather | **le grand-père** | [lə grah~ payr] |
| The uncle | **l'oncle** | [loh~-klə] |
| The cat | **le chat** | [lə shah] |
| The dog | **le chien** | [lə shyahn] |
| The book | **le livre** | [lə lee-vrə] |
| The telephone | **le téléphone** | [lə teh-leh-foh-nə] |
| The youngster | **le jeune** | [lə jøn] |

## Singular Feminine Nouns

The feminine singular noun uses the definite article « **la** ».

| English | French | Pronunciation |
|---|---|---|
| The person | **la personne** | [lah pehr-sohn] |
| The woman | **la femme** | [lah fahm] |
| The mother | **la mère** | [lah mayr] |
| The friend (female) | **l'amie** | [lah-mee] |
| The girl | **la fille** | [lah feey] |
| The sister | **la sœur** | [lah sør] |
| The grandmother | **la grand-mère** | [lah grah~ mayr] |

| English | French | Pronunciation |
|---|---|---|
| The aunt | **la tante** | [lah tah~-tə] |
| The cat (female) | **la chatte** | [lah shaht] |
| The dog (female) | **la chienne** | [lah shyayn] |
| The house | **la maison** | [lah may-zoh~] |
| The food | **la nourriture** | [lah noo-ree-tur] |
| The chair | **la chaise** | [lah shayz] |

Having established a preliminary understanding of the usage of noun genders, let's reinforce this knowledge through some hands-on practice! Are you prepared?

## Practice 2.1 Gender of Nouns

Instructions: What's the appropriate masculine or feminine form of the definite article (the) for each noun? And while you're at it, try translating the word to see if you remember the meaning!

1. _____ photo (f.)
2. _____ hôpital (m.)
3. _____ télévision (f.)
4. _____ programme (m.)
5. _____ système (m.)
6. _____ problème (m.)

7. _____ planète (f.)
8. _____ hôtel (m.)
9. _____ personne (f.)
10. _____ animal (m.)
11. _____ conversation (f.)
12. _____ téléphone (m.)

# 2.2 Plural Nouns and the Plural Definite Article

## Plural Nouns

So far, we've only covered singular nouns. That is, just one object, place, or thing. But what if you wanted to refer to multiple friends, not just one friend? Or many books, not just a single book? This is where plural nouns come in.

In English, we usually indicate that there is *more* than one thing by adding –s to the end of the word, like 'friends' or 'books'. In French, plurality is also indicated by modifying the ending of the word.

In French, plural nouns end in either an **–s** or **–x**.

Speak Abroad
Academy

If the French singular noun ends in EAU, AU, or EU, you'll add an –**x** to the end of the word. For example, with the nouns…

**tableau (picture)**   →   **tableaux**
**cheveu (hair)**      →   **cheveux**

However, there are always a few exceptions

**un pneu**    →   **des pneus**
**un landau**  →   **des landaus**
**bleu**       →   **bleus**

If the ending is AL, it will add –**aux.** For example…

**cheval (horse)**   →   **chevaux**

However, there are always a few exceptions

**un bal**      →   **des bals**
**un carnaval**  →   **des carnavals**

When it's not –**x,** the plural noun will end in –**s**. For example, when you want to indicate more than one friend, you would then use the word **amis**, and for more than one table, you would use **tables**.

**ami**    →   **amis**
**table**  →   **tables**

Fingers crossed, you're catching the rhythm of this dance by now!  If you're referring to multiple pencils, you'd use the word **crayons**. And for multiple mouths, you would use the word **bouches**.

You might be noticing that something is missing – the definite article. How do we say 'the tables' or 'the cities'?

Just like the nouns, the definite articles are also modified to indicate plurality.

The masculine definite article **le** becomes **les**.

The feminine definite article **la** becomes **les**.

For example…

**le** chien    →    **les** chiens
**la** maison    →    **les** maisons

---

Remember that in French, if we're referring to multiple people that consist of both females and males, we use the masculine plurality by default. So, you would use the term **les amis** when referring to your friends if your friends include female and male people.

To clarify…

**les amis** = male friends OR male friends + female friends

---

Keep in mind that, just like in English, we don't always need to use the definite article. In English, the definite article is the word 'the,' and in French, this is **le**, **la** (or **l'**) and **les**. So, when do you need to use the definite article?

First, let's just quickly go over what the point of the definite article is. Let's use an English example.

If you have a salad in your fridge that you really need to eat before it goes bad, you would say: 'I need to eat *the* salad.' Using the definite article indicates that you have a specific salad in mind. It's already there and it's just waiting to be eaten!

However, if you feel like you've been eating too much fast food lately, you might say: 'I need to eat *a* salad.' In this case, you don't have a specific salad in mind, you just need to eat any salad. That's why we call it the *definite* article, because there is more sureness and specificity implied.

These rules about when to use the definite article also apply to French – but a couple of extra ones are added on top. Let's summarize!

---

In French, the definite article (**le**, **la**, **les**) is used…

like English, to refer to a specific person or thing. **La femme d'Adam est Eve** (*Eve is Adam's woman*).

unlike English, to refer to something in a conceptual or broad sense. **J'aime la viande** (*I like meat*) or **J'aime la musique** (*I like music*).

unlike English, to refer to parts of your own body. **Je me suis cassé le bras** (*I broke my arm*).

---

     Nouns and articles

Now that we've built a preliminary foundation in the use of plural nouns, it's time for a little practice to really solidify that knowledge! Are you ready?

## Practice 2.2 Plural Nouns

**A. Write the plural version of each singular noun. When you finish, read each pair out loud.**

1. L'homme _____
2. L'amie _____
3. La conversation _____
4. L'animal _____
5. Le système _____

6. Le petit _____
7. La maison _____
8. Le train _____
9. La ville _____
10. Le médecin _____

**B. Write the singular version of each plural noun. When you finish, read each pair out loud.**

1. Les vérités _____
2. Les télévisions _____
3. Les mains _____
4. Les chiennes _____

5. Les crayons _____
6. Les filles _____
7. Les radios _____
8. Les salades _____

# 2.3    The Indefinite Article

Now that we've chatted about the definite article, it's time to meet its more mysterious cousin — the indefinite article. Curious to find out more? Let's dive into the world of indefinite articles together! Remember when we talked about the difference between 'I need to eat *the* salad' and 'I need to eat *a* salad'? As you can probably guess, it's in '*a* salad' where the indefinite article is used. We use the indefinite article to refer to a thing that is non-specific.

In English, the indefinite article is *a* or *an*. In French, the indefinite articles are…

Masculine, singular: **un** (*a/an*)
Masculine, plural: **des** (*some*)

Feminine, singular: **une** (*a/an*)
Feminine, plural: **des** (*some*)

For example:

**Une amie** (*a female friend*)   →   **des amies** (*some female friends*)
**Un garçon** (*a boy*)   →   **des garçons** (*some boys*)

To summarize, you only use the indefinite article (**un**, **une**, **des**) when:

⮕ You want to identify someone or something as part of a class or a group: **c'est un animal** (*it's an animal*).

⮕ You want to refer to something in a non-specific way: **Un bateau est fait pour naviguer** (*A boat is for sailing*) or **C'est une jeune femme** (*She's a young woman*).

## Quick Recap

| | MASCULINE SINGULAR NOUNS | MASCULINE PLURAL NOUNS | FEMININE SINGULAR NOUNS | FEMININE PLURAL NOUNS |
|---|---|---|---|---|
| **DEFINITE ARTICLES** | **Le** chien (the male dog) | **Les** chiens (the male dogs or the female and male dogs) | **La** chienne (the female dog) | **Les** chiennes (the female dogs) |
| **INDEFINITE ARTICLES** | **Un** chien (a male dog) | **Des** chiens (some male dogs or some female and male dogs) | **Une** chienne (a female dog) | **Des** chiennes (some female dogs) |

**Un** and **une** (both *a* and *an*) can mean *one* as well as *a* or *an*. You will understand which one it means based on the context. For example, **un** garçon (*a boy*) vs. J'achète **un** manteau (*I buy one coat*).

Now that we've laid the groundwork for handling plural nouns and indefinite articles, it's time to roll up our sleeves and put that knowledge into action! Ready for a bit of practice to make those concepts stick? Let's dive in and elevate that French fluency!

## Practice 2.3 Indefinite Articles

**A. Turn these singular nouns with indefinite articles into plural nouns with their indefinite articles.**

1. un grand-père : _____
2. une conversation : _____
3. un chien : _____
4. une femme : _____
5. un étudiant : _____

6. un médecin : _____
7. un hôtel : _____
8. un train : _____
9. un crayon : _____
10. une ville : _____

**B. Translate the following:**

1. The (male and female) students: _____
2. The planets: _____
3. A doctor: _____
4. Some photographs: _____
5. The language: _____
6. The tourists: _____
7. Some (male and female) friends: _____
8. A tomato: _____
9. The conversation: _____
10. Some truths: _____

**C. Complete the sentences with le, la, les, or un, une, des.**

1. _____ maison de Samuel.
2. J'ai trouvé (*I found*) _____ pièces de monnaie (*coins*).
3. C'est _____ tête (*head*) de François.
4. C'est _____ trace de pied (*footprint*).
5. Ce sont _____ amies de ma soeur. (*They are some friends of my sisters.*)
6. J'aime _____ poulet. (*I like chicken.*)
7. Je ramène _____ gâteau chez toi. (*I'm taking a cake to your house.*)
8. Samuel va acheter _____ boissons pour la fête. (*Samuel is buying the drinks for the party.*)

**D. Do you remember what these nouns are in English? Remember to translate them with the definite or indefinite article that precedes them.**

1. Le livre _____
2. La maison _____
3. Les fleurs _____
4. Le jeune garçon _____
5. Les frères _____
6. Le café _____
7. Le train _____
8. Les planètes _____
9. Un chat _____
10. Des chiens _____
11. Le téléphone _____
12. Les mains _____
13. Un programme _____
14. Des systèmes _____
15. Les livres _____
16. La ville _____

**E. Circle the right answer. You need to decide whether the article should be singular or plural:**

1. [ La / Les ] mère de Thomas est sympathique.
2. Je veux [ un / des ] livres pour apprendre.
3. Je veux [ les / une ] nouvelle télévision.
4. [ Le / Des ] chat est un animal indépendant.
5. Il a brisé (*he broke*) [ les / une ] fenêtre de la maison.
6. J'aime [ les / la ] fleurs.
7. J'ai parlé (*I spoke*) avec [ le / des ] directeur du collège.
8. Amélie a vu [ les / un ] chat.
9. Je mets (*I put*) [ les / une ] clés (*keys*) dans le sac (*purse*).

**F. Complete with the right definite or indefinite article (le/la/les/un/une/des).**

1. Washington est _____ ville aux États-Unis.
2. La rue Voltaire est _____ rue de ton village.
3. Paris est _____ capitale de la France.
4. _____ maison de Clara est grande.
5. _____ pape vit à Rome.
6. J'ai besoin de (*I need*) _____ veste (*jacket*) rouge.
7. As-tu _____ clés (*keys*) de la maison ?
8. J'ai vu (*I saw*) _____ grand lion (*lion*) au zoo (*zoo*).

Nouns and articles

Speak Abroad
Academy

We invite you to scan this "QR code"

**<u>By using the camera of your phone aiming at the
QR code and clicking on the link that appears</u>**

to access your bonus content:

SCAN TO CLAIM YOUR BONUSES

OR

ENTER THIS URL IN YOUR WEB BROWSER:

# bit.ly/speakfrwb

CHAPTER 3:

# DESCRIBING PEOPLE, PLACES, AND THINGS
## *THE BLACK CAT*

## 3.1  Singular Adjectives

Remember what a noun is? It's a person, place, or thing, like 'house' or 'table'.

Sometimes it isn't enough to simply mention the object or subject – sometimes, it's necessary to describe the object or subject. This is where adjectives come in. We use adjectives to describe the nouns we're talking about. For example, we could say that a person is beautiful and smart – or that a table is big or small.

In French, we usually put the adjective *after* the noun that we're describing, except when we're talking about:

⮑ Beauty – When something or someone is beautiful, pretty, or handsome, e.g. *beau* ('beautiful or handsome').

⮑ Age – When something or someone is young, new, or old, e.g. *jeune* ('young').

⮑ Goodness – When something is good or bad, e.g. *bon* ('good').

⮑ Size – When something or someone is small, big, long, or fat, e.g. *petit* ('small').

For example, to say 'the friendly cat', this would look like **le gentil chat.** As you can guess, the word **gentil** means friendly and it is the adjective.

You can remember this with the acronym BAGS.

However, in most other cases, the adjective goes after the noun.

Adjectives are also used to describe other qualities, like the nationality of something or someone. For example, to say 'French food', we would say **nourriture française.**

**Furthermore,** the ending of an adjective will also change depending on:

⮑ the gender of the noun;

⮑ the singularity or plurality of the noun.

Speak Abroad
Academy

So, if you have a feminine singular noun like **la photo** (*the photo*), you would need to use a feminine singular adjective like **jolie** (*beautiful*) to describe it. In this case, you would say **la jolie photo** to mean 'the beautiful photo'.

## Masculine Singular Forms of Adjectives

Here are some examples of adjectives for singular masculine nouns. Remember, some of these will go *before* the noun!

| English | French | Pronunciation |
|---|---|---|
| The tall student | **le grand étudiant** | [lə grah~ ay-tu-dyah~] |
| The short boy | **le petit garçon** | [lə pə-tee gahr-soh~] |
| The good brother | **le bon frère** | [lə boh~ frayr] |
| The bad dog | **le mauvais chien** | [lə moh-vay gahr-soh~] |
| The fat cat | **le gros chat** | [lə groh shah] |
| The thin uncle | **l'oncle mince** | [l'oh~-klə mɪns] |
| The friendly boy | **le gentil garçon** | [lə joh~-tee gahr-soh~] |
| The unfriendly teenager | **l'adolescent antipathique** | [lah-doh-lay-soh~ ah~-tee-pah-teek] |
| The small book | **le petit livre** | [lə pə-tee lee-vrə] |
| The hardworking grandfather | **le grand-père travailleur** | [lə gra~ payr trah-vah-yør] |
| The beautiful sofa | **le joli sofa** | [lə joh-lee soh-fa] |
| The old man | **le vieil homme** | [lə vee-ay ohm] |

**Feminine Singular Forms of Adjectives**

But what if you're not referring to a masculine noun? Sometimes, you need to describe a female student as tall, not just a male student! Notice how the endings of the adjectives change in the following list.

| English | French | Pronunciation |
|---|---|---|
| The tall (female) student | **la grande étudiante** | [lah grah~-də ay-tu-dyah~-tə] |
| The short girl | **la petite fille** | [lah pə-teet feey] |
| The kind sister | **la gentille sœur** | [lah bohn sør] |
| The bad (female) dog | **la mauvaise chienne** | [lah moh-vayz shyayn] |
| The fat (female) cat | **la grosse chatte** | [lah grohs shat] |
| The thin aunt | **la tante mince** | [lah tohta mɪns] |
| The friendly girl | **la gentille fille** | [lah joh~-tee feey] |
| The unfriendly (female) youngster | **l'adolescente antipathique** | [lah-doh-lay-soh~-tə ah~-tee-pah-teek] |
| The small house | **la petite maison** | [lah pə-teet may-zoh~] |
| The hardworking grandmother | **la grand-mère travailleuse** | [lah gra~ mayr trah-vah-yøz] |
| The beautiful city | **la jolie ville** | [lah joh-lee vil] |
| The old woman | **la vieille femme** | [lah vee-ay fahm] |

## Endings that Don't Change

Most often, you need to add « e » at the end of a masculine adjective to create the feminine version, unless there's already an « e » at the end.

**Le grand garçon** becomes **la grande fille**.
**Le jeune homme** becomes **la jeune femme**.

However, sometimes, you're lucky because you don't need to change the ending of an adjective. This makes it a little easier! For the following adjectives, the ending remains the same for masculine and feminine nouns.

Speak Abroad
Academy

| English | French | Pronunciation |
|---|---|---|
| The weak boy | **le faible garçon** | *[lə fay-blə gahr-soh~]* |
| The poor man | **le pauvre homme** | *[lə poh-vrə ohm]* |
| The loyal friend | **l'ami fidèle** | *[lah-mee fee-dayl]* |
| The difficult conversation | **la conversation difficile/ la difficile conversation** | *[lah koh~-vayr-sah-syoh~ dee-fee-seel]* |
| The friendly professor | **l'aimable professeur** | *[lay-mah-blə proh-fay-sør]* |
| The young girl | **la jeune fille** | *[lah jøn feey]* |

Ready to rock the world of singular masculine and feminine adjectives? Let's jump into practice, making these concepts your language allies and boosting your French fluency!

## Practice 3.1 Singular Adjectives

**A. Translate the English adjective into its French equivalent. Make sure it matches the noun.**

1. La _____ fille (tall)
2. Le _____ homme (poor)
3. Le chien _____ (loyal)
4. Le _____ homme (beautiful)
5. Le problème _____ (difficult)

6. Le _____ garçon (good)
7. L' _____ grand-père (happy)
8. Le livre _____ (interesting)
9. La _____ amitié (strong)
10. La main _____ (weak)

**B. Translate the English adjective into its French equivalent. Make sure it matches the noun.**

1. La _____ fille (short)
2. L' _____ nourriture (excellent)
3. La _____ ville (small)
4. Le _____ garçon (friendly) (hardworking)
5. Le _____ lieu (old)

6. Le _____ chat (bad)
7. L'amie _____ (intelligent)
8. La chienne _____ (loyal)
9. Le garçon _____
10. La _____ touriste (fat)

**C. Write the opposite adjectives to the one in the sentences below.**

1.  Le thème facile _____
2.  Le petit garçon _____
3.  Le mauvais restaurant _____
4.  La fille antipathique _____
5.  Le petit chien _____
6.  L'homme fort _____

# 3.2   Plural Form of Adjectives

Bet you saw this one coming, right? When the noun is plural and refers to multiple things, the adjectives must be modified to agree with the plurality.

When an adjective refers to more than one masculine noun, we add **–s** to the end of the adjective. For example...

**Grand**    →    **grands** (*tall*)

**Pauvre**    →    **pauvres** (*poor*)

If the noun you're describing is feminine, then instead you'll add **–es** to the end of the adjective. For example…

**Grande**    →    **grandes** (tall)

Watch out for some exceptions! For instance, some words ending with **–x** do not change.

**Un homme heureux**    →    **des hommes heureux**

Remember this rule: if the French singular noun ends in EAU, AU, or EU, you'll add an **–x** to the end of the word.

This works for adjectives too!

**Un bel homme**    →    **de beaux hommes**

Let's practice this!

## Practice 3.2 Plural Adjectives

**A. Write the plural form of each of the following nouns and adjectives.**

1. La grande tomate _____
2. Le petit homme _____
3. Le chien intelligent _____
4. La fille forte _____
5. La personne travailleuse _____
6. La petite ville _____
7. Le chat mince _____
8. La femme heureuse _____
9. Le livre difficile _____
10. L'excellente nourriture _____

**B. Complete the sentence with the correct form of the adjectives:**

1. Les _____ livres (excellent)
2. La grand-mère _____ (travailleur)
3. La _____ ville(beau)
4. Les _____ livres (petit)
5. Les _____ sofas (joli)
6. Les _____ sœurs (bon)
7. Les _____ chats (gros)
8. Les enfants _____ (sympathique)

# 3.3  Adjectives of Nationality

As mentioned earlier, nationalities are also adjectives. They describe that a person or thing originates from a specific country.

Like the other adjectives we've discussed, they are also modified depending on the gender of the noun and plurality.

For example, we would say…

**The man is Tunisian.**  →  L'homme est tunisien.
**The men are Tunisian.**  →  Les hommes sont tunisiens.

And for feminine nouns, we would say…

**The woman is French.** → La femme est française.
**The women are French.** → Les femmes sont françaises.

Notice how these rules work just like they do for the other adjectives! So, how do we refer to other nationalities in French?

| English | French | Pronunciation |
| --- | --- | --- |
| French | **français** | *[frah~-say]* |
| English | **anglais** | *[ah~-glay]* |
| American | **américain** | *[ah-may-ree-kahn]* |
| Spanish | **espagnol** | *[ays-pahn-yohl]* |
| German | **allemand** | *[ah-leh-mah~]* |
| Italian | **italien** | *[ee-tah-lyahn]* |
| Portuguese | **portugais** | *[pohr-tu-gay]* |
| Japanese | **japonais** | *[jah-ph-nay]* |
| Chinese | **chinois** | *[shee-nwah]* |
| Tunisian | **tunisien** | *[tu-neez-yahn]* |

> **Tip:** In French, you must capitalize the names of nationalities when they are used as nouns, but not when they are used as adjectives.

Having established an understanding of the usage of adjectives of nationality, let's reinforce this knowledge through some hands-on practice! Are you ready?

## Practice 3.3 Nationality

**Write the nationality next to each noun, making it match in gender and number.**

1. La statue de la liberté est _____
2. La Tour Eiffel est _____
3. Big Ben est _____
4. La Tour de Pise est _____
5. Le musée du Prado est _____
6. Angela Merkel est _____

Speak Abroad
Academy

# 3.4 Describing a Person

In French, there's more than one way to write a descriptive sentence – just like in English. You can say 'the intelligent woman' or you can say 'the woman is intelligent.'

So far, we've only discussed how to say sentences like 'the intelligent woman', i.e. **la femme intelligente.** Now, let's try a different way of using these descriptors.

To say a singular someone or something *is* something, you use the French word **est.** This means that 'the woman is intelligent' would become « **la femme est intelligente** ».

Of course, you don't always have to specify 'the woman', you can also use pronouns to indicate who you're talking about. In this case, just replace the noun with the pronoun. To simply say 'she is intelligent', you translate this to « **elle est intelligente** ».

Thankfully, the words 'is' and **est** are only different by two letters, so this should be somewhat easy to remember! You'll also be glad to hear that you use the word **est** no matter if you're talking about a feminine or masculine noun. For example, 'he is intelligent' would be « il **est intelligent** ».

Now, let's jazz up our descriptive skills by diving into hands-on practice with adjectives when describing someone! Are you up for the fun challenge?

## Practice 3.4 Describing People

### A. Which adjectives are the most appropriate for each sentence?

1. La fille est [ vieille / jeune ]
2. Le bébé est [ petit / grand ]
3. Le livre est [ intéressant / bruyant ]
4. Le garçon est [ drôle / délicieux ]
5. L'étudiant est [ mauvais / intelligent ]
6. Le chien est [ loyal / pauvre ]

### B. Choose which adjective is most appropriate depending on the gender agreement.

1. La femme est [ intelligente / intelligent ]
2. L'homme est [ grande / grand ]

3. L'étudiant est [ français / française ]
4. Le chat est [ gros / grosse ]
5. La fleur est [ belle / beau ]
6. La mère est [ gentil / gentille ]
7. Le père est [ anglaise / anglais ]
8. L'oncle est [ vieux / vieille ]

**C. Translate the following into French:**

1. Marc is French: _____
2. Anna is English: _____
3. The boy is tall: _____
4. The girl is intelligent: _____
5. The man is kind: _____
6. The woman is pretty: _____

**D. Do you remember where these famous people are from?**

1. Napoléon Bonaparte est _____
2. Kim Kardashian est _____
3. Daniel Craig est _____
4. Marco Polo est _____
5. Coco Chanel est _____
6. La reine Elizabeth II est _____

Describing people, places, and things

## CHAPTER 4:

# MORE DESCRIPTORS

*THE YELLOW BRICK ROAD*

## 4.1   More Adjectives

It's time to pause the rulebook and dive into a symphony of new words! Let's unleash the power of French adjectives, and watch as your vocabulary transforms into a kaleidoscope, painting the world, people, and experiences with vibrant hues of expression. By learning more French adjectives, you'll be able to describe the world, the people around you, and the experiences you have in greater detail. So, are you ready to splash some linguistic colors? Let the wordplay begin!

We will begin with some useful everyday adjectives that you'll need to know.

### Essential Everyday Adjectives

| English | French | Pronunciation |
|---|---|---|
| Fast | **rapide** | [rah-peed] |
| Slow | **lent** | [loh~] |
| Expensive | **cher** | [shayr] |
| Constant | **constant** | [koh~-stah~] |
| Famous | **célèbre** | [selɛbʁ] |
| Long | **long** | [loh~] |
| Short | **court** | [koor] |
| Young | **jeune** | [jøn] |
| Elderly | **vieux** | [vyø] |
| Pretty | **beau** | [boh] |
| Ugly | **laid** | [lay] |
| Happy | **joyeux** | [jwah-yø] |
| Sad | **triste** | [treest] |
| Rich | **riche** | [reesh] |

| English | French | Pronunciation |
|---------|--------|---------------|
| New | **nouveau** | [noo-voh] |
| Blond | **blond** | [bloh~] |
| Dark-haired | **brun** | [brahn] |
| Delicious | **délicieux** | [day-lees-yø] |

You might be wondering what these adjectives would look like in a sentence. Let's use them with some nouns we used in prior chapters.

**Le problème facile**          (the easy problem)
**La moto rapide**              (the fast motorcycle)
**La douleur constante**        (the constant pain)
**La fille célèbre**            (the famous girl)
**La joyeuse femme**            (the happy woman)
**L'homme triste**              (the sad man)
**Le garçon brun**              (the dark-haired boy)
**La délicieuse nourriture**    (the delicious food)
**La courte leçon**             (the short lesson)
**Le long train**               (the long train)

In a nutshell, these adjectives add color and detail to familiar nouns. Now, it's your turn to play with these combinations and paint your own linguistic canvas. Ready to give it a go? Take out your notepad because practice makes perfect!

## Diving into the Colors

Colors in French, just like other adjectives, play a crucial role. Apply the rules you've mastered for adjectives to colors as well — treat them the same way, positioning them after the noun. Let's keep the color palette of your French language vivid and vibrant!

Explore the table below to acquaint yourself with fundamental colors in French. If you're an art enthusiast accustomed to the world of colors, you might recognize a few. French is renowned in the realm of artist's paints and makeup products, making it a familiar language for color aficionados.

## Basic Colors

| English | French | Pronunciation |
|---------|--------|---------------|
| White | **blanc** | [blah~] |
| Black | **noir** | [nwahr] |
| Red | **rouge** | [rooj] |
| Blue | **bleu** | [blø] |
| Yellow | **jaune** | [john] |
| Green | **vert** | [vayr] |
| Gray | **gris** | [grees] |
| Pink | **rose** | [rohz] |
| Brown | **marron** | [mah-roh~] |
| Orange | **orange** | [oh-rah~-j] |

We've seen that adjectives that already end with an **–e** do not change with their gender. It's the same for colors. Here, let's take a look!

| English | French (m.) | French (f.) |
|---------|-------------|-------------|
| White | **blanc** | **blanche** |
| Black | **noir** | **noire** |
| Red | **rouge** | **rouge** |
| Blue | **bleu** | **bleue** |
| Yellow | **jaune** | **jaune** |
| Green | **vert** | **verte** |
| Gray | **gris** | **grise** |
| Pink | **rose** | **rose** |
| Brown | **marron** | **marron** |
| Orange | **orange** | **orange** |

Nope, this is no mistake. Marron doesn't change with its gender. And it doesn't change with plural either. Quite impressive!

**une maison marron – des maisons marron**

Additionally, here are more examples of how to use colors with a noun:

**La planète rouge**    (*the red planet*)
**Le crayon noir**    (*the black pencil*)
**Le chat blanc**    *(the white cat)*
**Le sofa jaune**    (*the yellow sofa*)
**La chaise verte**    (*the green chair*)
**La moto bleue**    (*the blue motorcycle*)
**La maison rose**    (*the pink house*)
**La chienne marron**    (*the brown dog*)

To modify these colors for plurality or multiple nouns, add **–s** (if it's masculine) or **–es** (if it's feminine) to the end of each adjective. For example…

**Les planètes rouges**    (*the red planets*)
**Les crayons noirs**    (*the black pencils*)
**Les chats blancs**    *(the white cats)*
**Les sofas jaunes**    (*the yellow sofa*)
**Les chaises vertes**    (*the green chairs*)
**Les motos bleues**    (*the blue motorcycles*)
**Les maisons roses**    (*the pink houses*)
**Les chiennes marron**    (*the brown dogs*)

## Practice 4.1 Adjectives

**A. Find the right adjective for the following nouns according to whether the noun is masculine or feminine.**

1. La voiture est _____ (nouvelle / nouveau)
2. La femme est _____ (joyeuse / joyeux)
3. L'étudiant est _____ (bon / bonne)
4. Le chien est _____ (gros / grosse)
5. L'homme est _____ (petite / petit)
6. Le garçon est _____ (méchant /méchante)
7. Le livre est _____ (vieux / vieille)
8. La maison est _____ (chère / cher)

9. Le bébé est _____ (grand / grande)

10. La fille est _____ (lent / lente)

11. Le chat est _____ (bruyant / bruyante)

12. Le train est _____ (long / longue)

**B. Complete the following phrases translating the color adjective in English to French.**

1. La fleur _____ (yellow)

2. La maison _____ (blue)

3. La chaise _____ (orange)

4. La main _____ (white)

5. La chatte _____ (black)

6. Le crayon _____ (gris)

7. Le sofa _____ (green)

8. Le téléphone _____ (pink)

9. Le chien _____ (brown)

10. La tomate _____ (red)

**C. Complete the sentences in French below by claiming the opposite of what the first part of the sentence says. English example: The cat is slow and the dog is fast.**

1. L'homme est lent et la femme est _____

2. Le chat est noir et la chienne est _____

3. La voiture est grande et l'enfant est _____

4. L'enfant est gros et la fille est _____

5. Le père est vieux et la mère est _____

6. La grand-mère est riche et le grand-père est _____

**D. All these people and things are complete opposites. Complete the sentences in French.**

1. Rachel est petite et jeune. Thomas est _____.

2. Emily est belle et riche. Sarah est _____.

3. La maison est nouvelle et grande. La voiture est _____.

4. Jennifer est triste et lente. Stuart est _____.

5. L'examen est difficile. Le jeu vidéo est _____.

## 4.2 Demonstrative Adjectives

We've talked mainly about common adjectives so far. Now, let's talk about demonstrative adjectives. You've probably noticed that we're throwing around some very official linguistic terminology here. Let me just say that although it's important for you to be introduced to official terms like 'demonstrative adjective', you don't have to remember them *as long as you remember the rule itself.*

So, let's talk about demonstrative adjectives.

These are words like 'this' or 'that', which draw attention to specific nouns (singular or plural). You know what purpose they serve in English, and it's essentially the same in French.

When we use these words, they go *before* the noun, just like in English, and they also change if we're talking about multiple nouns. This is like the difference between 'this' and 'these'. For example, you would say **ce chien** for 'this dog' and **ces chiens** for 'these dogs'.

And of course, they also need to be modified if you're talking about a feminine noun, like for example, **cette maison** (this house) and **ces maisons** (these houses).

| this | ce (m.) | [sə] | cette (f.) | [sayt] |
|---|---|---|---|---|
|  | cet (+ vowel) (m.) | [sayt] |  |  |
| these | ces (m.) | [say] | ces (f. pl.) | [say] |

Now let's see if you're with me so far:

### Practice 4.2 Demonstrative Adjectives

A. **Beatriz and her friend go shopping. Check out what they say about the clothes, using the demonstrative adjectives in their correct form. Use est (*is*) or sont (*are*) depending on whether the subject is singular or plural.**

Example: robe (dress) / rouge (red) → **cette robe est rouge**.

1. manteau (coat) / beau → _____

2. chaussures (shoes) / chères → _____

3. chemise (shirt) / douce (soft) → _____

4. bottes (boots) / élégantes (elegant) → _____

5. chapeau (hat) / propre (clean) → _____

More descriptors

**\*Très** is an adverb that means **very**. Adverbs go before adjectives and verbs. Check out some more adverbs here:

| | | |
|---|---|---|
| **très** (*very*) | + adjective/adverb | Ces fleurs sont **très** belles. <br> *(Those flowers are very beautiful)* |
| **beaucoup** (*a lot*) | + verb | Samuel voyage **beaucoup**. <br> *(Samuel travels a lot)* |
| **assez** (*quite*) | + adjective/adverb/verb | Elle marche **assez** rapidement <br> *(She walks quite fast)* |
| **peu** (*not a lot*) | + adjective/adverb/verb | Martin mange **peu** . <br> *(Martin doesn't eat a lot)* |
| **trop** (*too much*) | + adjective/adverb/verb | Amélie parle **trop**. <br> *(Amélie talks too much)* |

**B. Complete these sentences with ce, (cet), cette, or ces.**

1. Qui (*Who*) est _____ (*this*) médecin ? (*This*) _____ médecin est un cardiologue (*cardiologist*).
2. _____ (*This*) planète est très grande.
3. _____ (*This*) maison est belle.
4. _____ (*This*) train est grand.
5. _____ (*This*) moto est nouvelle.
6. _____ (*These*) jeunes sont sympathiques.
7. _____ (*This*) étudiant est jeune.
8. _____ (*These*) filles sont intelligentes

# 4.3 Describing People and Adjectives in the Plural Form

Remember when we talked about using **est** to describe a singular noun? Like, for example, **la femme est intelligente** to say 'the woman is intelligent'?

It also becomes necessary to describe plural nouns in the same way. In English, 'is' becomes 'are' when we're talking about plural nouns, like in the sentence 'the books are boring'. We've done some of this in French already, but let's get more acquainted with these rules.

In French, **est** becomes **sont**.

Instead of...

>**Il est** : *he (m.) is*
>**Elle est** : *she (f.) is*

You would say...

>**Ils sont** : *they (m.) are*
>**Elles sont** : *they (f.) are*

Just like **est**, you use the word **sont** regardless of whether the noun is feminine or masculine.

For example:

**They (a group of men) are thin.** → Ils sont minces.
**They (a group of women) are intelligent.** → Elles sont intelligentes.

Now, you know how to say 'he/she/it is' and 'they are'! Try and practice this with different adjectives.

## Vocabulary: The Neighborhood

Time to expand your vocabulary! Let's look at some nouns that you'll encounter in your typical neighborhood, town, and city.

| English | French | Pronunciation |
|---|---|---|
| Tree | **arbre (m.)** | [ahr-brə] |
| Flower | **fleur (f.)** | [flør] |
| Street | **rue (f.)** | [ru] |
| Post office | **Poste (f.)** | [post] |
| Bakery | **boulangerie (f.)** | [boo-lah~-jə-ree] |
| Supermarket | **supermarché (m.)** | [su-payr-mahr-shay] |
| Office | **bureau (m.)** | [bu-roh] |
| Car | **voiture (f.)** | [vwah-tur] |
| Movie theatre | **cinéma (m.)** | [tay-ah-trə] |
| Park | **parc (m.)** | [pahrk] |
| Garden/yard | **jardin (m.)** | [jahr-dahn] |

More descriptors

| English | French | Pronunciation |
|---|---|---|
| School | **école (f.)** | *[ay-kohl]* |
| College/university | **université (f.)** | *[u-nee-vehr-see-tay]* |
| Train station | **gare (f.)** | *[lah gahr]* |
| Subway station | **station de métro (f.)** | *[lah stahs-yoh~]* |
| Church | **église (f.)** | *[ay-gleez]* |
| Airport | **aéroport (m.)** | *[ah-eh-roh-pohr]* |
| Museum | **musée (m.)** | *[mu-zay]* |
| Bar | **bar (m.)** | *[bahr]* |
| Restaurant | **restaurant (m.)** | *[ray-stoh-rah~]* |
| Building | **bâtiment (m.)** | *[bah-tee-moh~]* |
| Shop | **boutique (f.)** | *[boo-teek]* |

Now that we understand how to use adjectives in the plural form to describe people, it's time to put ourselves to the test!

## Practice 4.3 Describing Nouns

**A. Imagine you're showing your friend around your block from your car. Point out some places of interest, completing the sentences with the right form of *this*: ce, cette, ces, cet.**

1. _____ maison est très grande.
2. _____ bâtiment (*building*) est la Poste (*post office*) et _____ arbre est très vieux.
3. _____ rue (*street*) est nouvelle et _____ chiens sont dangereux (*dangerous*).
4. _____ église (*church*) est vieille.

**B. Rewrite these sentences using the right form of the demonstrative adjective est or sont (depending on whether the subject is singular or plural).**

1. Ces bâtiments _____ très vieux.
   (*These buildings are very old.*)
2. L'aéroport _____ nouveau, mais les gares _____ vieilles.
   (*The airport is new but the trains stations are old.*)

3. Le musée _____ près du supermarché.
   *(The museum is next to the supermarket.)*

4. Les arbres _____ grands et le jardin _____ petit.
   *(The trees are big and the garden is small.)*

5. La boulangerie _____ mon endroit préféré.
   *(The bakery is my favorite place.)*

6. Les boutiques ici _____ américaines. Les boutiques là bas _____ françaises.
   *(The shops here are American. The shops there are French.)*

7. Les parcs _____ beaux.
   *(The parks are beautiful.)*

8. L'école _____ proche de l'université.
   *(The school is next to the university.)*

9. Les fleurs _____ roses.
   *(The flowers are pink.)*

10. Les livres _____ chers parce que la bibliothèque _____ vieille.
    *(The books are expensive because the library is old.)*

---

**Common Mistake**: When using the word **personne**, avoid using a masculine adjective, even if the sex of the person you are referring to is male. **Personne** always agrees with a **feminine adjective**:

X     Alain est une bo**n** personne.

✓     Alain est une bon**ne personne**.

X     Martin est une personne travailleur.

✓     Martin est une **personne** travailleu**se**.

X     Samuel est une genti**l** personne.

✓     Samuel est une genti**lle personne**.

---

More descriptors

## THE VERB ÊTRE

*TO BE OR NOT TO BE*

## 5.1 Present Tense of Être

I hope you remember the words **est** and **sont**. They mean 'is' and 'are', which are essentially the same thing, but one is singular and the other is plural. The French words **est** and **sont** are all rooted in the same verb être, which means 'to be'.

In English, we use the words 'is' and 'are' for basically everything. You use it to say both 'the car is red' (description) and 'the car is here' (location), even though you're describing pretty different types of qualities. It's a very useful verb, and it's just as useful in French.

However, there is one big difference!

In French, there are more than two variations of this important word.

You already know **est** and **sont** ('is' and 'are'), which can be used to say **il/elle est** (he/she/it is) and **ils/elles sont** (they are). But what if you wanted to say 'we are' or 'I am'? To refer to different pronouns, you'll need to make modifications.

Let's take a look at these modifications!

| Être *to be* | | | |
|---|---|---|---|
| je | **suis** | nous | **sommes** |
| tu | **es** | vous | êtes |
| il | | ils | |
| elle | **est** | elles | **sont** |

Here are some examples of how we use these words in sentences.

| **I am intelligent.** | → | Je suis intelligent. |
|---|---|---|
| **I am a cat.** | → | Je suis un chat. |
| **I am young.** | → | Je suis jeune. |

| | | |
|---|---|---|
| **We are intelligent.** | → | Nous sommes intelligents. |
| **We are cats.** | → | Nous sommes des chats. |
| **We are happy.** | → | Nous sommes heureux. |
| | | |
| **You are intelligent** (inf.). | → | Tu es intelligent. |
| **You are a cat** (inf.). | → | Tu es un chat. |
| **You are old** (inf.). | → | Tu es vieux. |
| | | |
| **You are intelligent** (form.). | → | Vous êtes intelligent. |
| **You are a cat** (form.). | → | Vous êtes un chat. |
| **You are beautiful** (form.). | → | Vous êtes beau. |
| | | |
| **You all are intelligent** (pl.). | → | Vous êtes intelligents. |
| **You all are cats** (pl.). | → | Vous êtes des chats. |
| **You all are funny** (pl.). | → | Vous êtes drôles. |
| | | |
| **They are intelligent** (m., co-ed.). | → | Ils sont intelligents. |
| **They are cats** (m., co-ed.). | → | Ils sont des chats. |
| **They are poor** (m., co-ed.). | → | Ils sont pauvres. |
| | | |
| **They are intelligent** (f.). | → | Elles sont intelligentes. |
| **They are cats** (f.). | → | Elles sont des chattes. |
| **They are kind** (f.). | → | Elles sont gentilles. |

## Profession

We also use these verbs to indicate someone's profession. However, you'll notice that, in French, this works differently from English.

In English, you would say, 'I am *a* doctor' or 'You are *a* teacher'.

In French, you would say, '*Je suis médecin*' or '*Tu es professeur*'.

When indicating someone's profession in French, omit the definite and indefinite article. You simply *are* the profession.

The table below introduces some French words for other professions so you can get used to practicing subject pronouns with the verb être.

## Common Professions

| English | French | Pronunciation |
|---|---|---|
| Doctor | **médecin** | [may-də-sahn] |
| Teacher | **professeur** | [proh-feh-sør] |
| Painter | **peintre** | [pahn-trə] |
| Chef | **chef** | [chef] |
| Engineer | **ingénieur** | [ah-jayn-yør] |
| Artist | **artiste** | [ahr-teest] |
| Baker | **boulanger** | [boo-lah~-jay] |
| Secretary | **secrétaire** | [sehk-ray-tayr] |
| Waiter | **serveur** | [sehr-vør] |
| Nurse | **infirmier** | [ahn-feerm-yay] |
| Writer | **écrivain** | [ayk-ree-vahn] |
| Police officer | **policier** | [poh-lees-yay] |
| Lawyer | **avocat** | [ah-voh-kah] |
| Manager | **gérant** | [jay-rah~] |
| Fire fighter | **pompier** | [pohm-pee-ay] |
| Cashier | **caissier** | [kays-yay] |
| Pharmacist | **pharmacien** | [fahr-mah-syahn] |
| Driver | **chauffeur** | [shoh-før] |

Ready to take the stage with your linguistic performance? Time to put yourself to the test!

## Practice 5. Être

**A. Read the following dialogue in 'New in the City' and then answer the questions.**

**New in the City / (Nouveau dans la ville)**

THOMAS:     Excusez-moi, êtes-vous d'ici ? Je suis perdu.

ADELINE:     Non, je suis une touriste.

| THOMAS: | Êtes-vous française ? |
| ADELINE: | Oui, je suis française. |

| THOMAS: | Oh ! Je suis français aussi. Mais mon ami Paul est anglais. |
| ADELINE: | Je suis perdue aussi. New York, c'est grand ! |

| THOMAS: | Vous êtes perdue aussi ? Ah ! Voici une carte ! |

**Glossary:**

d'ici: from here

perdu: lost

touriste: tourist

aussi: too/also

mais: but

mon ami: my friend

voici: here

carte: map

1. Who is lost? (Qui est perdu ?) _____
2. Who is French? (Qui est français ?) _____
3. Who is English? (Qui est anglais ?) _____
4. Why are they lost? (Pourquoi sont-ils perdus ?) _____
5. What did they find to help them? (Qu'est-ce qu'ils ont trouvé pour les aider ?) _____

**B. Where are these famous people from? Use the word est to say what nationality they are.**

Anglais/e (English)

Italien/ne (Italian)

Américain/e (American)

Français/e (French)

Portugais/e (Portuguese)

Autrichien/ne (Austrian)

Espagnol/e (Spanish)

Mexicain/e (Mexican)

Allemand/e (German)

**Example**: David Beckham est anglais.

1. Luciano Pavarotti _____
2. Frida Kahlo _____
3. Johnny Depp _____
4. Albert Einstein _____
5. Coco Chanel _____
6. Rafael Nadal _____
7. Cristiano Ronaldo _____
8. Paul McCartney _____
9. Arnold Schwarzenegger _____

**C. Complete the following sentences with the appropriate form of the verb être. Pay attention to the subjects and subject pronouns that they follow.**

1. Nous _____ heureux d'être ici. (*We are happy to be here.*)
2. Tu _____ mon meilleur ami. (*You are my best friend. – inf.*)
3. Les filles _____ en train de jouer en haut. (*The girls are playing upstairs.*)
4. Je _____ dentiste. Tu _____ médecin. (*I am a dentist. You are a doctor.*)
5. Mon mari _____ très grand. (*My husband is very tall.*)
6. Les enfants _____ en train de jouer dehors. (*The boys are playing outside.*)
7. Ils _____ des nouveaux étudiants. (*They are new students.*)
8. Nous _____ en train de manger au parc. (*We are eating at the park.*)
9. Aujourd'hui, elle _____ au travail. (*Today, she is at work.*)
10. Aujourd'hui, il _____ en train de jouer au football. (*Today, he is playing football.*)
11. Excusez-moi, Madame, vous _____ très belle. (*Excuse me, Madame, you are very beautiful.*)
12. Vous (pl.) _____ des invités magnifiques. (*You all are fantastic guests.*)
13. Je _____ au supermarché. (*I am at the supermarket.*)
14. Melissa _____ dans la voiture. (*Melissa is in the car.*)
15. La vache _____ dans le jardin! Elle _____ en train de manger les fleurs! (*The cow is in the garden! She is eating the flowers!*)
16. Ils _____ les meilleurs danseurs au monde. (*They are the best dancers in the world.*)
17. Vous (pl.) _____ invités à ma soirée. (*You all are invited to my party.*)
18. Les femmes _____ très rapides. (*The women are very fast.*)
19. Tu _____ ma fille préférée. (*You are my favorite daughter.*)
20. Maman, je _____ ta fille unique! (*Mom, I'm your only daughter!*)

**D. Add the correct subject pronouns and forms of the verb être next to the following characters.**

**Example:** <u>She</u> is slow. _Elle est lente._

1. <u>We are</u> happy. _____ _contents._
2. <u>They (m.) are</u> very intelligent. _____ _très intelligents._
3. <u>I am</u> tired. _____ _fatigué._
4. <u>You (inf.) are</u> the best. _____ _le meilleur._
5. <u>You (form.) are</u> at the bank. _____ _à la banque._
6. <u>We are</u> old. _____ _vieux._
7. <u>They (f.) are</u> young and beautiful. _____ _jeunes et belles._
8. <u>They (m.) are</u> outside. _____ _dehors._
9. <u>I am</u> at the museum. _____ _au musée._
10. <u>They (co-ed.) are</u> at school today. _____ _à l'école aujourd'hui._
11. <u>You (inf.) are</u> taller than me. _____ _plus grand que moi._
12. <u>You (plur.) all are</u> very loud. _____ _très bruyants._

**E. Write the following English sentences in French.**

1. Anna is at the museum. _____.
2. We are outside. _____.
3. Elsa and Jane are at school. _____.
4. They _(co-ed.)_ are at the bank. _____.
5. He is at the supermarket. _____.
6. She is very loud. _____.
7. We are in the car. _____.
8. You _(inf.)_ are happy. _____.
9. I am young and beautiful. _____.
10. You _(f.)_ are very intelligent. _____.
11. George is old. _____.
12. You _(pl.)_ are at the supermarket. _____.

**F. Fill the blanks with the missing French words, using everything we've learned in the book so far.**

1. Anna _____ au supermarché. (Anna <u>is</u> at the supermarket.)

2. Nous _____ dehors dans _____. (We <u>are</u> outside in <u>the car.</u>)

3. Elle _____ dans le jardin. Il _____ dans _____ (She <u>is</u> in the garden. He <u>is</u> in <u>the house.</u>)

4. Je _____ serveur. Elle _____ secrétaire. (I <u>am</u> a waiter. She <u>is</u> a secretary.)

5. Peter _____ français. Et Emily? _____ aussi! (Peter <u>is</u> French. And Emily? <u>She is French</u> too!)

6. Tu _____ *(inf.)* belle et je _____ intelligent. (You <u>are</u> pretty and I <u>am</u> intelligent.)

**G. Read the following French conversation and see if you can identify who is from where.**

ALAN :        Je suis anglais. Et toi ? Es-tu français ?

BILL :        Non, je suis américain. Elle est anglaise !

ALAN :        Qui ?

CHRISTINE :        Moi !

DANIEL :        Moi aussi. Nous sommes anglais.

CHRISTINE :        Oui, je vis à Londres. Il vit à Manchester.

ALAN :        Qui est français?

CHRISTINE :        Emily ?

EMILY :        Non, je suis espagnole ! Frédéric ?

FRÉDÉRIC :        Oui ?

EMILY :        Vous êtes français !

FRÉDÉRIC :        Oui, oui, je suis français. Je vis à Paris. Gina et Haruki sont français aussi.

EMILY :        Non, Frédéric. Ils sont japonais !

**Glossary:**

Qui : who                          Il vit : He lives

Je vis : I live                      Londres : London

1. ALAN: _____        5. EMILY: _____

2. BILL: _____        6. FREDERIC: _____

3. CHRISTINE: _____        7. GINA: _____

4. DANIEL: _____        8. HARUKI: _____

**H. The people from the previous dialogue are getting to know each other a little better. Read the following French conversation and identify which profession everyone has.**

| | |
|---|---|
| ALAN : | Où travailles-tu ? |
| EMILY : | À l'hôpital. Je suis médecin. |
| HARUKI : | Je suis médecin aussi. Et toi ? |
| ALAN : | Je suis chauffeur. |
| FRÉDÉRIC : | Oh, c'est ta voiture ? La voiture rouge ? |
| ALAN : | Oui ! C'est ma voiture ! C'est ton vélo ? |
| FRÉDÉRIC : | Oui, c'est mon vélo ! |
| BILL : | Ma femme est chauffeur aussi. |
| ALAN : | Et toi ? |
| BILL : | Je suis peintre ! |
| FRÉDÉRIC : | Oh, fantastique ! Je suis écrivain. |
| GINA and DANIEL : | Nous sommes écrivains aussi ! |
| BILL : | Et toi, Christine ? Tu es calme ! |
| CHRISTINE : | Devine ! Qui cuisine ce soir ? |
| BILL : | Oh ! Tu es cheffe cuisinière ! |
| CHRISTINE : | Correct, Bill ! |

**Glossary:**

Où travailles-tu ? : Where do you work?
Hôpital : hospital
Ta voiture : your car
Ma voiture : my car
Ton vélo : your bicycle

Mon vélo : my bicycle
Calme : quiet
Devine : guess
Cuisine : cook
Ce soir : tonight

1. ALAN: _____     5. EMILY: _____
2. BILL: _____     6. FREDERIC: _____
3. CHRISTINE: _____     7. GINA: _____
4. DANIEL: _____     8. HARUKI: _____

Speak Abroad
Academy

## I. Translate the following French sentences into English.

1. Cette robe est jolie et très chère.

   _____

2. L'homme dans la voiture est médecin.

   _____

3. Les professeurs sont très intelligents. Et les étudiants ? Ils sont intelligents aussi !

   _____

4. Cette maison-ci est grande et cette maison-là est petite.

   _____

5. Ces chiens sont vieux, mais ils sont rapides.

   _____

6. Les hommes sont à une soirée et les femmes sont au restaurant.

   _____

7. Aujourd'hui, la fille est fatiguée. Elle est très travailleuse.

   _____

8. La femme française est une avocate. L'homme américain est un chauffeur. Ils sont amis.

   _____

9. Cette chemise-ci est noire et jolie. Cette chemise-là est blanche et laide, mais ce n'est pas cher !

   _____

10. Le chat est dans le jardin. Oh non ! La vache est dans le jardin aussi.

    _____

11. Il est très calme. Il est pharmacien et la pharmacie est calme.

    _____

**CHAPTER 6:**

# THE VERB AVOIR

*I HAVE NINETY-NINE PROBLEMS AND FRENCH ISN'T ONE*

## 6.1 Present Tense of Avoir

In the previous chapter, you discovered the most important verb of all, meaning 'to be'. The next verb that's essential for you to learn is *avoir*, which means 'to have'. This useful verb indicates that you possess something, though this is not always physical. In fact, *avoir* is also used to say how old you are, what you need, and form other tenses.

But for now, let's focus on constructing simple sentences with *avoir*.

| Avoir *to have* | | | |
|---|---|---|---|
| j' | **ai** | nous | **avons** |
| tu | **as** | vous | **avez** |
| il | | ils | |
| elle | **a** | elles | **ont** |

Notice something interesting about the first-person singular conjugation of *avoir*? That's right, *je* becomes *j'* because the next letter begins with a vowel. This happens a lot in French. So instead of saying *je ai* (incorrect!), you say *j'ai* to say 'I have'.

Here are some examples of how to use *avoir* in sentences.

| | | |
|---|---|---|
| **I have a dog.** | → | J'ai un chien. |
| **I have a big house.** | → | J'ai une grande maison. |
| **I have an expensive dress.** | → | J'ai une robe chère. |
| **We have a dog.** | → | Nous avons un chien. |
| **We have a big house.** | → | Nous avons une grande maison. |
| **We have an important meeting.** | → | Nous avons une réunion importante. |

| | | |
|---|---|---|
| **You have a dog** (inf.). | → | Tu as un chien. |
| **You have a big house** (inf.). | → | Tu as une grande maison. |
| **You have a new television** (inf.). | → | Tu as une nouvelle télévision. |
| | | |
| **You have a dog** (form.). | → | Vous avez un chien. |
| **You have a big house** (form.). | → | Vous avez une grande maison. |
| **You have a black umbrella** (form.). | → | Vous avez un parapluie noir. |
| | | |
| **You all have a dog** (pl.). | → | Vous avez un chien. |
| **You all have a big house** (pl.). | → | Vous avez une grande maison. |
| **You all have a lot to do today** (pl.). | → | Vous avez beaucoup de choses à faire aujourd'hui. |
| | | |
| **They have a dog.** | → | Ils ont un chien. |
| **They have a big house.** | → | Ils ont une grande maison. |
| **They have a beautiful car.** | → | Ils ont une jolie voiture. |
| | | |
| **They have a dog** (f.). | → | Elles ont un chien. |
| **They have a big house** (f.). | → | Elles ont une grande maison. |
| **They have a delicious cake** (f.). | → | Elles ont un gâteau délicieux. |

## Everyday Objects

I think it's time to get ready to sprout new French words! Let's add a splash of excitement to your vocabulary palette and watch it blossom. Here are some everyday objects that you can practice using *avoir* with.

## Essential Everyday Objects

| English | French | Pronunciation |
|---|---|---|
| Computer | **ordinateur (m.)** | [ohr-dee-nah-tør] |
| Mobile phone | **téléphone portable (m.)** | [tay-lay-phohn pohr-tah-blə] |
| Newspaper | **journal (m.)** | [joor-nahl] |
| Bag | **sac (m.)** | [sahk] |
| Scarf | **écharpe (f.)** | [ay-sharp] |
| Keys | **clés (f.)** | [klay] |
| Cup | **verre (m.)** | [vayr] |

| English | French | Pronunciation |
|---|---|---|
| Bottle | **bouteille (f.)** | *[boo-tay]* |
| Money | **argent (m.)** | *[ahr-joh~]* |
| Note | **billet (m.)** | *[bee-yay]* |
| Passport | **passeport (m.)** | *[pass-pohr]* |
| Notebook | **carnet (m.)** | *[kahr-nay]* |
| Pen | **stylo (m.)** | *[stee-loh]* |
| Umbrella | **parapluie (m.)** | *[pah-rah-plwee]* |
| Sunglasses | **lunettes de soleil (f.)** | *[luh-nayt də soh-lay]* |

## Family Members

Of course, we can't forget some of the most important people that we *have*. Our family members!

| English | French | Pronunciation |
|---|---|---|
| Family | **famille (f.)** | *[fah-mee]* |
| Mother | **mère (f.)** | *[mayr]* |
| Father | **père (m.)** | *[payr]* |
| Sister | **sœur (f.)** | *[sør]* |
| Brother | **frère (m.)** | *[frayr]* |
| Grandmother | **grand-mère (f.)** | *[grah~ mayr]* |
| Grandfather | **grand-père (m.)** | *[grah~ payr]* |
| Uncle | **oncle (m.)** | *[oh~-klə]* |
| Aunt | **tante (f.)** | *[tah~-tə]* |
| Husband | **époux (m.)** | *[ay-poo]* |
| Wife | **épouse (f.)** | *[ay-pooz]* |
| Daughter | **fille (f.)** | *[feey]* |
| Son | **fils (m.)** | *[fees]* |
| Cousin | **cousin (m.)** | *[koo-zahn]* |
| Niece | **nièce (f.)** | *[nee-yes]* |
| Nephew | **neveu (m.)** | *[nə-vø]* |

With *avoir* firmly grasped, let's dive into hands-on practice! Ready to flex those French language muscles? Let's get started!

## Practice 6.1 Present Tense of Avoir

**A. Write the appropriate form of avoir for the following sentences. This time let's bring the definite article (*le, la*) back into the mix!**

1. _____ une idée intéressante. (*We have an interesting idea.*)
2. _____ une voiture blanche. (*I have a white car.*)
3. _____ la plus belle écharpe. (*You have the most beautiful scarf – inf.*)
4. _____ un billet de train. (*I have a train ticket.*)
5. _____ une jolie sœur. (*She has a pretty sister.*)
6. _____ trois ordinateurs. (*They have three computers – co-ed.*)
7. _____ un chien drôle. (*He has a funny dog.*)
8. _____ une mère gentille. (*They have a kind mother – f.*)
9. _____ une grande famille. (*You have a big family – form.*)
10. _____ une fille intelligente et un grand fils. (*We have an intelligent daughter and a tall son.*)

**B. Based on the context of the sentence, identify whether to use être or avoir to fill in the blanks. Make sure to match the subject pronoun in the parentheses and conjugate the verb accordingly!**

1. Aujourd'hui, _____ fatigué. (*I*)
2. _____ un rendez-vous important. (*You – form.*)
3. _____ une jolie épouse. _____ heureux. (*He*)
4. _____ une grande maison. _____ riche. (*She*)
5. Moi? _____ médecin. (*I*)
6. _____ un gâteau délicieux. (*They – co-ed.*)
7. _____ médecins. (*We*)
8. _____ deux chiens. (*I*)
9. _____ jeune ! _____ un téléphone portable. (*You – inf.*)
10. _____ gentilles. Et _____ belles aussi! (*They – f.*)
11. _____ une vieille voiture. (*We*)

## C. Fill in the blanks and finish the French translations of these English sentences, using the correct form of avoir.

1. *I'm running late! I have an appointment at noon.*
   Je suis en retard ! _____ un rendez-vous à midi.

2. *They have a big family. That's why they have a big house (co-ed.)*
   _____ une grande famille. C'est pour ça qu' _____ une grande maison.

3. *She has three cats and he has four dogs.*
   _____ trois chats et _____ quatre chiens.

4. *You have a kind brother (form.).*
   _____ un gentil frère.

5. *They have too many cars (f.).*
   _____ trop de voitures.

6. *We have a son who is a doctor.*
   _____ un fils qui est médecin.

7. *I have a pink flower. It's for my mother.*
   _____ une fleur rose. C'est pour ma mère.

8. *You have a newspaper? You're an old man (inf.)!*
   _____ un journal ? Tu es un vieil homme !

## D. Paul and Francine are getting to know each other better. Read the following French dialogue and answer the questions.

PAUL : As-tu une grande famille ?

FRANCINE : Oui. J'ai trois sœurs et quatre frères. Et toi ?

PAUL : J'ai une petite famille. Je suis enfant unique.

FRANCINE : As-tu des cousins ?

PAUL : Oui, j'ai un cousin.

FRANCINE : Wow, tu as une petite famille !

PAUL : Oui. Mais j'ai cinq chiens. Ils sont ma famille aussi.

FRANCINE : Je comprends. Mes chats sont ma famille aussi.

### Glossary

| | |
|---|---|
| Trois : three | Ma famille : my family |
| Quatre : four | Je comprends : I understand |
| Cinq : five | Mes chats : my cats |
| Enfant unique : only child | |

1. How many sisters does Francine have? _____
   (*Combien de sœurs a Francine ?*)
2. How many brothers does Francine have? _____
   (*Combien de frères a Francine ?*)
3. How many siblings does Paul have? _____
   (*Combien de frères et sœurs a Paul ?*)
4. Who has one cousin? _____
   (*Qui a un seul cousin ?*)
5. Who has dogs? How many? _____
   (*Qui a des chiens ? Combien ?*)
6. Who has cats? _____
   (*Qui a des chats ?*)

## 6.2   Other Uses for Avoir

In French, you use 'I have' to indicate more than just your possessions. It's also used to say that you are hungry or thirsty. For example…

| | | |
|---|---|---|
| **I have hunger ('I am hungry').** | → | J'ai faim. |
| **I have thirst ('I am thirsty').** | → | J'ai soif. |
| **We have hunger ('We are hungry').** | → | Nous avons faim. |
| **She has thirst ('She is thirsty').** | → | Elle a soif. |
| **He has hunger ('He is hungry').** | → | Il a faim. |
| **You have thirst ('You are thirsty').** | → | Tu as soif. |

You get the idea! In French, you don't say that you *are* thirsty or hungry. You say that you *have* thirst or hunger, which means you always use **avoir** in these scenarios.

### Expressing Age

Another way that French differs from English is how they express age. Again, they don't say they *are* a certain number of years old. Instead, they say they *have* a certain number of years. This looks like…

**I have _____ years ('I am _____ years old').** → J'ai _____ ans.
**She has _____ years ('She is _____ years old').** → Elle a _____ ans.
**He has _____ years ('He is _____ years old').** → Il a _____ ans.

Even when you're asking for someone's age, keep in mind that you're asking how many years they *have*.

**How old are you?** (inf.) → Quel âge as-tu ?
**How old are you?** (form.) → Quel âge avez-vous ?

**How old is she?** → Quel âge a-t-elle ?
**How old is he?** → Quel âge a-t-il ?

**How old are they?** (m., co-ed.) → Quel âge ont-ils ?
**How old are they?** (f.) → Quel âge ont-elles ?

Have you noticed that sometimes, you add *a-t-* after 'avoir' ? It's only to help with the pronunciation when the connection between vowels is difficult to make.

Quel âge ont-ils ?  Quel âge a-t-il ?

To fill in the blanks above, let's learn some numbers!

## Numbers

| English | French | Pronunciation |
|---------|--------|---------------|
| zero | **zéro** | [zay-roh] |
| one | **un** | [ahn] |
| two | **deux** | [dø] |
| three | **trois** | [trwah] |
| four | **quatre** | [kahtr] |
| five | **cinq** | [sahnk] |
| six | **six** | [sees] |
| seven | **sept** | [set] |
| eight | **huit** | [weet] |
| nine | **neuf** | [nøf] |
| ten | **dix** | [dees] |

| eleven | **onze** | *[oh~z]* |
| twelve | **douze** | *[dooz]* |
| thirteen | **treize** | *[trayz]* |
| fourteen | **quatorze** | *[kah-tohrz]* |
| fifteen | **quinze** | *[kahnz]* |
| sixteen | **seize** | *[sayz]* |
| seventeen | **dix-sept** | *[dee set]* |
| eighteen | **dix-huit** | *[deez weet]* |
| nineteen | **dix-neut** | *[deez nøf]* |
| twenty | **vingt** | *[vahn]* |
| | | |
| twenty-one | **vingt-et-un** | *[vahnt ay ahn]* |
| twenty-two | **vingt-deux** | *[vahn dø]* |
| twenty-three | **vingt-trois** | *[vahn trwah]* |
| twenty-four | **vingt-quatre** | *[vahnt kahtr]* |
| twenty-five | **vingt-cinq** | *[vahnt sahnk]* |
| twenty-six | **vingt-six** | *[vahnt sees]* |
| twenty-seven | **vingt-sept** | *[vahnt set]* |
| twenty-eight | **vingt-huit** | *[vahnt weet]* |
| twenty-nine | **vingt-neuf** | *[vahnt nøf]* |
| thirty | **trente** | *[troh~t]* |
| | | |
| thirty-one | **trente-et-un** | *[troh~t ay ahn]* |
| thirty-two | **trente-deux** | *[troh~t dø]* |
| thirty-three | **trente-trois** | *[troh~t trwah]* |
| thirty-four | **trente-quatre** | *[troh~t kahtr]* |
| thirty-five | **trente-cinq** | *[troh~t sahnk]* |
| thirty-six | **trente-six** | *[troh~t sees]* |
| thirty-seven | **trente-sept** | *[troh~t set]* |
| thirty-eight | **trente-huit** | *[troh~t weet]* |
| thirty-nine | **trente-neuf** | *[troh~t nøf]* |
| forty | **quarante** | *[kah-roh~t]* |

Now that you have a good idea of how the French words for numbers are modified as they increase, let's get a little higher!

| | | |
|---|---|---|
| fifty | **cinquante** | [sahn-koh~t] |
| sixty | **soixante** | [swah-soh~t] |
| seventy | **soixante-dix** | [swah-soh~t dees] |
| eighty | **quatre-vingts** | [kahtr vahn] |
| ninety | **quatre-vingt-dix** | [kahtr vahn dees] |
| one hundred | **cent** | [soh~] |
| two hundred | **deux cents** | [dø soh~] |
| three hundred | **trois cents** | [trwah soh~] |
| four hundred | **quatre cents** | [kahtr soh~] |
| five hundred | **cinq cents** | [sahnk soh~] |
| | | |
| one thousand | **mille** | [meel] |
| ten thousand | **dix mille** | [dee meel] |
| one million | **un million** | [ahn meel-yoh~] |
| ten million | **dix millions** | [dee meel-yoh~] |
| one billion | **un milliard** | [ahn meel-yahr] |
| ten billion | **dix milliards** | [dee meel-yahr] |
| infinity | **infini** | [ahn-fee-nee] |

Now let's reinforce this knowledge through some hands-on practice! Are you ready?

## Practice 6.2 Age

**A. Write the French translations of these English sentences using the correct form of avoir to express age.**

**Example**: I'm twenty years old. _J'ai vingt ans._

1. I'm twenty-five years old. _____
2. I'm thirty years old. _____
3. I'm thirty-seven years old. _____
4. I'm forty years old. _____

The verb avoir

5. I'm forty-one years old. _____

6. I'm ninety years old. _____

**B. Now. Let's make things a little bit harder! Following the same instructions as the prior section, translate these English sentences into French. This time, we're using more than just the first-person singular pronoun.**

**Example:** We are twenty years old. _Nous avons vingt ans._

1. She is twenty years old. _____

2. We are fifteen years old. _____

3. They (co-ed.) are eighty-five years old. _____

4. They (f.) are eighty-six years old. _____

5. You (_inf._) are twenty-nine years old. _____

6. You (_form._) are sixty years old. _____

7. I am thirty-eight years old. _____

8. He is one hundred years old. _____

**C. Now, let's combine what you learned about expressing age with the two most important verbs we've learned so far. Read the following French sentences and declare in French whether these people are old (_vieux/vieille_) or young (_jeune_). Remember to match the subject pronoun!**

**Example:** J'ai cent ans. _Je suis vieux._

1. Elle a deux ans. _____

2. Il a quatre-vingt-dix ans. _____

3. Nous avons dix ans. _____

4. Nous avons quatre-vingt-cinq ans. _____

5. Ils ont quatre-vingt-un ans. _____

6. J'ai huit ans. _____

7. Tu as quatre ans. _____

8. Les femmes ont soixante-dix-neuf ans. _____

9. La fille a onze ans. _____

10. L'homme a quatre-vingt-dix-neuf ans. _____

# 6.3 Expressing Quantity

As you're aware, we have alternative methods for conveying quantity. Rather than resorting to numerical expressions, opting for terms such as 'a lot' or 'many' provides a nuanced approach. While French offers a plethora of such expressions, we will focus on the most important ones for the moment.

## Essential Words Expressing Quantity

| English | French | Pronunciation |
|:---:|:---:|:---:|
| a lot / many | **beaucoup** | [boh-koo] |
| too much / too many | **trop** | [troh] |
| several | **plusieurs** | [pluhz-yør] |
| a little / a bit | **un peu** | [ahn pø] |
| less | **moins** | [mwahn] |
| more | **plus** | [pluhs] |

In sentences, this looks like…

| | | |
|---|---|---|
| **He eats a lot.** | → | Il mange beaucoup. |
| **She has too many cats.** | → | Elle a trop de chats. |
| **They have too many children.** | → | Ils ont trop d'enfants. |
| **I have several books.** | → | J'ai plusieurs livres. |
| **We have a little time.** | → | Nous avons un peu de temps. |
| **I have more cars than Sally…** | → | J'ai plus de voitures que Sally… |
| **…but I have less friends than Sally.** | → | … mais j'ai moins d'amis que Sally. |

Now, let's practice everything you've learned!

## Practice 6.3 Quantity

### A. Translate these French sentences into English.

1. Marie a dix chats. Elle a trop de chats !

   _____

2. J'ai plus d'enfants que Jennifer.

   _____

3. Il a beaucoup d'oncles et de tantes. Ils sont trop bruyants.

   _____

4. Ils ont un peu d'argent.

   _____

5. Nous avons trop de problèmes.

   _____

6. Nina a moins d'amis que Natasha.

   _____

7. James a dix dollars. Jim a quinze dollars. Jim a plus d'argent que James.

   _____

8. Daniel et Emily ont trente euros. Nous avons moins d'argent que Daniel et Emily.

   _____

### B. Read the following sentences and indicate in French who has more or less than the other.

**Example:** Anna has twenty dollars. Abigail has twenty-five dollars. Abigail <u>a plus d'argent qu'Anna</u>.

1. Bill has two cats. Bob has six cats.
   Bill _____.
2. Charlie has three daughters. Chris has five daughters.
   Chris _____.
3. Daniel has fifteen dollars. Daisy has eleven dollars.
   Daisy _____.
4. Emily has thirty books. Eric has sixty-one books.
   Eric _____.
5. Freddie has five dogs. I have one dog.

   _____.
6. I have twelve cars. George has two cars.

   _____.

**C. Read the following French dialogue between two competitive classmates. Answer the questions at the end using the glossary.**

ISABELLE : Ma mère a beaucoup d'argent. Elle est très riche.

LUCY : Vraiment ? Mon père aussi a beaucoup d'argent. Il a six voitures.

ISABELLE : Ma mère a plus de voitures que ton père. Elle a neuf voitures.

LUCY : Mon père a un avion.

ISABELLE : Ma mère a deux avions. Nous voyageons beaucoup.

LUCY : Je vais à Paris chaque mois.

ISABELLE : Je vais à Paris chaque semaine !

LUCY : J'achète beaucoup de robes quand je suis à Paris. J'ai deux cents robes.

ISABELLE : J'ai deux mille robes !

LUCY : Tu mens !

ISABELLE : Non, c'est toi qui mens !

## Glossary

Vraiment : really?

Un avion : a plane

Nous voyageons : we travel

Je vais : I go

Chaque mois : every month

Chaque semaine : every week

J'achète : I buy

Quand : when

Tu mens : you're lying

1. How many cars does Lucy's father have? _____
   (*Combien de voitures possède le père de Lucy ?*)

2. How many cars does Isabelle's mother have? _____
   (*Combien de voitures possède la mère d'Isabelle ?*)

3. Whose parent has the most planes? _____
   (*Le parent de qui a-t-il le plus d'avions ?*)

4. Who goes to Paris more often? _____
   (*Qui va le plus souvent à Paris ?*)

5. How many dresses does Lucy have? _____
   (*Combien de robes a Lucy ?*)

6. How many dresses does Isabelle have? _____
   (*Combien de robes a Isabelle ?*)

**CHAPTER 7:**

# FRENCH DEMONSTRATIVES

*THERE'S A SMILE ON MY FACE; IT'S A GREAT DAY TO
LEARN FRENCH!*

## 7.1 French Demonstratives

Don't be intimidated by the big word! Demonstratives are used to state that something exists. When we say 'There is...' or 'There are...' we are using demonstratives to communicate what is present.

In French, to state 'there is' or 'there are' you begin a sentence with **il y a.** And you'll be relieved to hear that it's the same whether you're talking about a singular noun or a plural noun! It's in the words that follow **il y a** that you indicate whether you're talking about one thing or many things.

For example...

| | | |
|---|---|---|
| **There is a car outside.** | → | Il y a une voiture dehors. |
| **There are flowers outside.** | → | Il y a des fleurs dehors. |

### Introduction to Prepositions of Place

To make these demonstratives a little bit more exciting, let's learn some prepositions. Prepositions of place indicate the exact location of something. We'll learn some more later, but for now, let's learn the most important ones.

**Essential Prepositions of Place**

| English | French | Pronunciation |
|---|---|---|
| at | **à/(au if in front of masculine noun)** | *[ah]/[oh]* |
| behind | **derrière** | *[dehr-yayr]* |
| in/inside | **dans** | *[dah~]* |
| in front | **devant** | *[də-vah~]* |
| on | **sur** | *[suhr]* |
| under | **sous** | *[soo]* |

Here are some example sentences...

| | | |
|---|---|---|
| **She's at the house.** | → | Elle est à la maison. |
| **There is a cow in the garden.** | → | Il y a une vache dans le jardin. |
| **The cat is behind the car.** | → | Le chat est derrière la voiture. |
| **A boy is in front of the house.** | → | Un garçon est devant la maison. |
| **The book is under the table.** | → | Le livre est sous la table. |
| **The keys are on the table.** | → | Les clés sont sur la table. |

Now that we have a preliminary understanding of prepositions, it's time to put that knowledge to the test. Are you ready?

## Practice 7.1 Demonstratives

**A. Translate the following sentences into French using what you just learned about *il y a* and prepositions of place. For now, let's just focus on singular nouns.**

1. There's a flower in the garden. _____
2. There's a computer on the table. _____
3. There's a woman in front of the car. _____
4. There's a cat behind the house. _____
5. There's a girl under the table. _____

**B. Now, let's bring in some plural nouns and adjectives.**

1. There are women in the garden. _____
2. There are keys on the table. _____
3. There are three cats under the car. _____
4. There is a tall man outside. _____
5. There are five tall men outside. _____
6. There are red and yellow flowers in the garden. _____

## 7.2   More Demonstratives

We've covered how to say 'there is...' and 'there are...' but what if you want to make a different kind of declaration? Instead of saying 'he is...' or 'she is...' sometimes you want to state that *it* is something.

This is where ***c'est*** and ***ce sont*** come in.

Here's how they are used!

| | | |
|---|---|---|
| **It's a beautiful day.** | → | C'est une belle journée. |
| **It's terrible.** | → | C'est terrible. |
| **It's a blue sofa.** | → | C'est un sofa bleu. |
| **It's my mother's car.** | → | C'est la voiture de ma mère. |

And if you're talking about multiple nouns, you use **ce sont.**

| | | |
|---|---|---|
| **They are noisy dogs.** | → | Ce sont des chiens bruyants. |
| **These are black shoes.** | → | Ce sont des chaussures noires. |
| **These are red flowers.** | → | Ce sont des fleurs rouges. |
| **These are my father's socks.** | → | Ce sont les chaussettes de mon père. |

However, in French **c'est** and **ce sont** also work for people.

'She's my mother' can be the same as:

> **'This is my mother'** → C'est ma mère.

'They're my parents' can be the same as:

> **'These are my parents'** → Ce sont mes parents.

Hopefully, you're getting the idea! So, how do you know when to use **c'est** and when to use **il y a**? It's pretty simple. When you're using **c'est,** it's to directly point out something that is right there in front of you. For example, if a plane flies by, you might go, 'It's a plane!' In French this would be: 'C'est un avion !'

On the other hand, with **il y a** you're simply stating that something exists or that something is happening. However, you're not pointing at it and saying: 'There it is!'

## Household Places and Objects

Since we're learning about demonstratives and you now know about prepositions of place, let's learn how to use different places and objects in a house. These words are very helpful when trying to indicate where something is! We've learned some of these words in sentences already, but we'll list them in the following table anyway so you don't forget:

| English | French | Pronunciation |
|---|---|---|
| Basement | sous-sol (m.) | [soo sohl] |
| Bathroom | salle de bain (f.) | [sahl də bahn] |
| Bedroom | chambre (f.) | [shohm-brə] |
| Dining room | salle à manger (f.) | [sahl ah mah~-jay] |
| Garage | garage (m.) | [gah-rahj] |
| Garden | jardin (m.) | [jahr-dahn] |
| Kitchen | cuisine (f.) | [kwee-zeen] |
| Living room | salon (m.) | [sah-loh~] |
| Office | bureau (m.) | [buh-roh] |
| | | |
| Basket | panier (m.) | [pahn-yay] |
| Bed | lit (m.) | [lee] |
| Car | voiture (f.) | [vwah-tuhr] |
| Chair | chaise (f.) | [shayz] |
| Door | porte (f.) | [pohrt] |
| Floor | sol (m.) | [sohl] |
| Table | table (f.) | [tah-blə] |
| Sofa | sofa (m.) | [soh-fah] |
| Sink | lavabo (m.) | [lah-vah-boh] |
| Shower | douche (f.) | [doosh] |
| Television | télévision (f.) | [tay-lay-veez-yoh] |
| Wall | mur (m.) | [muhr] |
| Window | fenêtre (f.) | [fə-nay-trə] |

And just like that we are ready for practice! Don't worry, you can also go back in case you don't recall something.

French demonstratives

Speak Abroad
Academy

## Practice 7.2 Household Vocabulary

**A. Translate these French sentences into English using your new household vocabulary words.**

1. Les murs sont blancs.

2. La maison est petite, mais le jardin est grand.

3. J'aime la cuisine. Elle est belle et neuve.

4. Elle est dans le salon.

5. Nous sommes dans le bureau.

6. La famille est dans la salle à manger.

7. La voiture noire est dans le garage. La voiture rouge est dehors.

8. La femme est dans la salle de bains.

**B. Now let's bring in more demonstratives!**

1. La maison est grande. Il y a huit chambres et quatre salles de bain.

2. C'est une belle journée. Il y a des fleurs dans le jardin.

3. Il y a un chat dans le panier.

4. Il y a des livres sur le sol.

5. Il y a des voitures rouges dehors.

6. Il y a un chat noir devant la maison.

C. **Now let's make things even harder using everything we've learned in the book so far.**

1.  J'ai deux chats et deux chiens. Les chats sont sur le lit. Les chiens sont dans le jardin.

    _____

2.  Je suis chauffeur. J'ai trois voitures dans le garage. Une est noire. Deux sont rouges.

    _____

3.  Caroline est une fille sympathique. Elle a trente amis et ils sont sympathiques aussi.

    _____

4.  Il y a un grand homme dans le garage. C'est mon père. Et la femme sympathique dans la cuisine ? C'est ma mère.

    _____

5.  La femme du restaurant est vieille. Elle a quatre-vingt-six ans et elle a huit filles.

    _____

6.  Ces chaussures bleues sont neuves. Et ces chaussures vertes sont neuves aussi. J'ai trop de chaussures.

    _____

## 7.3   The Verb *Aller*

We've covered how to say you *are* and you *have*. Now, it's time to get a little more active. The verb *aller* means 'to go'. It's used to indicate movement, relocation, or your intention to relocate.

| Aller *to go* | | | |
|---|---|---|---|
| je | **vais** | nous | **allons** |
| tu | **vas** | vous | **allez** |
| il | | ils | |
| elle | **va** | elles | **vont** |

Here are some example sentences using ***aller.***

| | | |
|---|---|---|
| **I'm going to the museum.** | → | Je vais au musée. |
| **You're going to school today** (inf.). aujourd'hui. | → | Tu vas à l'école |

**You're going to France with Marie** (form.).  → Vous allez en France avec Marie.

**We're going to the supermarket.**  → Nous allons au supermarché.

**He is going to university.**  → Il va à l'université.

**She is going to the restaurant with her friend.**  → Elle va au restaurant avec son amie.

**They are going to the bank** (m., co-ed.).  → Ils vont à la banque.

**They are going to work** (f.).  → Elles vont au travail.

---

**Tip:** When the place you're referring to is a feminine noun, you say *Je vais à __la banque__* (I'm going to the bank). However, if you're referring to a masculine noun, you say *Je vais __au musée__*.

---

Gear up! Time to put into practice what we have learned!

## Practice 7.3 Aller

**A. Practice using *aller* with the different subject pronouns. For now, we'll keep it simple and talk about going to the park.**

1. _____ au parc. *(I'm going to the park.)*
2. _____ au parc. *(She's going to the park.)*
3. _____ au parc. *(He's going to the park.)*
4. _____ au parc. *(We are going to the park.)*
5. _____ au parc. *(You are going to the park – inf.)*
6. _____ au parc. *(You are going to the park – form.)*
7. _____ au parc. *(You are going to the park – pl.)*
8. _____ au parc. *(They are going to the park – m., co-ed.)*
9. _____ au parc. *(They are going to the park – f.)*

**B. Let's make things harder. Practice *aller* with different subject pronouns, but this time, let's throw some other locations into the mix.**

1. _____ au supermarché. *(You are going to the supermarket – inf.)*

2. _____ dans la chambre. *(He's going to the bedroom.)*

3. _____ au bar. *(They are going to the bar – f.)*

4. _____ à la boutique. *(I'm going to the shop.)*

5. _____ au bureau. *(You are going to the office – form.)*

6. _____ au jardin. *(She's going to the garden.)*

7. _____ à la boulangerie. *(They are going to the bakery – co-ed./m.)*

8. _____ au musée. *(We are going to the museum.)*

9. _____ au restaurant. *(You are going to the restaurant – pl.)*

10. _____ à la banque. *(I'm going to the bank.)*

**C. Let's make the sentences even trickier. Translate these French sentences into English.**

1. C'est une belle journée. Nous allons au parc.

   _____

2. Le supermarché est derrière la boulangerie.

   _____

3. Je suis dans le jardin et tu vas au travail.

   _____

4. La femme dans la voiture va à la banque.

   _____

5. Emily et Daniel vont au musée avec leurs amis.

   _____

6. Ma mère est à la maison. Mon père va au supermarché.

   _____

7. La famille va au restaurant.

   _____

8. Il va au bar dans sa nouvelle voiture.

   _____

9. Il y a un chien devant le restaurant.

   _____

10. Je vais à la maison ! Il y a une vache dehors.

   _____

Speak Abroad
Academy

## Other Ways of Using *Aller*

The verb ***aller*** is incredibly useful. You can even use it to indicate how you're doing. In English, this would be like if someone asked you, 'How's it going?' and you responded with 'It's going well'.

In French, this looks like...

| | | |
|---|---|---|
| **How's it going?** | → | Comment ça va ? |
| **Is your mother doing well?** | → | Est-ce que ta mère va bien ? |
| **Are they doing well?** | → | Vont-ils bien ? |

And you would answer...

| | | |
|---|---|---|
| **It's going well.** | → | Ça va bien. |
| **She's doing well.** | → | Elle va bien. |
| **We're doing well.** | → | Nous allons bien. |
| **They're doing well** (co-ed.). | → | Ils vont bien. |

Time to practice!

## Practice 7.4 Correct Sentences

**A. Let's see if you can spot whether these French sentences are grammatically correct or not. Pay attention to the conjugations, subject pronouns, articles, and word choices. If the sentence is correct, place a tick next to it. If it's wrong, place an X there instead.**

1. _____ Je allons bien.
2. _____ Je vais chez le médecin demain.
3. _____ Ce sont un beau chien.
4. _____ Ces femmes me plaisent, ils sont belles.
5. _____ Nous allons à l'école demain.
6. _____ Vous avons un examen.
7. _____ Le chien va bien.
8. _____ Les chats sont à la maison.
9. _____ La vache est dans le jardin.
10. _____ Il a médecin.

**B. For all the grammatically incorrect sentences in the previous exercise, write the corrections below.**

1. _____

2. _____

3. _____

4. _____

5. _____

**C. Likewise, let's try to choose the correct word in parentheses. Remember, there's only one right answer!**

1. Le chat [ va / vont ] dans la maison.

2. La voiture [ est / sont ] dans le garage.

3. Les filles [ a / ont ] des jolies robes.

4. Vous [ a / avez ] beaucoup d'argent.

5. Nous [ vont / allons ] au parc avec Marie.

6. Elle [ a / va ] un nouveau parapluie.

Speak Abroad
Academy

( CHAPTER 8: )

# MORE IMPORTANT VERBS
*DO AS I DO*

## 8.1  Present Tense of *Faire*

**You're still with me, yeah? Okay good!** Let's learn some more important verbs. *Faire* is an incredibly useful verb that allows you to say 'to do' or 'to make'. It's used very often to convey many kinds of expressions. It's also helpful when we're talking about activities and hobbies, like going shopping, exercising, and so on.

| Faire *to do / to make* | | | |
|---|---|---|---|
| je | **fais** | nous | **faisons** |
| tu | **fais** | vous | **faites** |
| il | | ils | |
| elle | **fait** | elles | **font** |

We can use *faire* in sentences like the following:

| | | |
|---|---|---|
| **I'm making a cake.** | → | Je fais un gâteau. |
| **I'm shopping.** | → | Je fais du shopping. |
| **She's cycling.** | → | Elle fait du vélo. |
| **She does sports.** | → | Elle fait du sport. |
| **He's doing his homework.** | → | Il fait ses devoirs. |
| **He's making the bed.** | → | Il fait le lit. |
| **You're making a cake** (inf.). | → | Tu fais un gâteau. |
| **We do photography.** | → | Nous faisons de la photographie. |
| **They are making a cake** (co-ed.). | → | Ils font un gâteau. |

Buckle up, there's a practice exercise coming up!

## Practice 8.1 *Faire*

**A. To get used to this new verb, let's practice using different conjugations of *faire* with this sentence about making the bed.**

1. _____ le lit. (*You are making the bed – inf.*)
2. _____ le lit. (*I'm making the bed.*)
3. _____ le lit. (*We are making the bed.*)
4. _____ le lit. (*They are making the bed – co-ed.*)
5. _____ le lit. (*He is making the bed.*)
6. _____ le lit. (*They are making the bed – f.*)
7. _____ le lit. (*She is making the bed.*)
8. _____ le lit. (*You are making the bed – form.*)

**B. Now, let's work on some slightly more complex sentences using *faire*. Translate the following into English.**

1. Nous faisons un gâteau dans la cuisine.

   _____

2. La grande femme fait de l'exercice dans le jardin.

   _____

3. Les deux amis font de la photographie dans le parc.

   _____

4. L'homme gentil fait la vaisselle.

   _____

5. Emily et Erica sont dans les magasins. Elles font du shopping.

   _____

# 8.2   Talking About the Weather with *Faire*

As we mentioned earlier, *faire* is a very useful adjective. It's also used to talk about the weather in an impersonal way. We use *faire* because the weather is constantly *doing* something; it's not just one fixed state. Here's how we use *faire* in a sentence to talk about the weather...

| | | |
|---|---|---|
| **The weather is good.** | → | Il fait beau. |
| **The weather is bad.** | → | Il fait mauvais. |
| **The weather is cold.** | → | Il fait froid. |
| **The weather is hot.** | → | Il fait chaud. |

However, we don't use *faire* to describe all kinds of weather. For example...

**It's snowing.** → Il neige.
**It's raining.** → Il pleut.
**It's windy.** → Il y a du vent.

## Weather and Climate Vocabulary

In order to describe the weather better, here are some new vocabulary words. Remember which one's you're supposed to use with *faire*.

| English | French | Pronunciation |
|---------|--------|---------------|
| Weather | **météo (f.)** | [may-tay-o] |
| Cold | **froid** | [frwah] |
| Hot | **très chaud** | [tray shoh] |
| Warm | **chaud** | [shoh] |
| Sunny | **ensoleillé** | [oh~-soh-lay-ay] |
| Rain | **pluie (f.)** | [plwee] |
| Clouds | **nuages (m.)** | [nuh-ahj] |
| Snow | **neige (f.)** | [nayj] |
| Storm | **tempête (f.)** | [tohm-payt] |
| Wind | **vent (m.)** | [voh~] |
| Thunder | **tonnerre (m.)** | [tohn-nayr] |
| Lightning | **éclair (m.)** | [ayk-layr] |
| Damp | **humide** | [uh-meed] |
| Dry | **sec** | [sayk] |
| Wet | **mouillé** | [moo-yay] |

## Practice 8.2 Weather

**A. Let's practice some basic sentences regarding the weather. Read what the following characters are wearing and determine whether it's cold (*il fait froid*), it's hot (*il fait chaud*), or it's raining (*il pleut*).**

1. Paula is wearing a raincoat (*Paula porte un manteau imperméable*).
   _____

2. Thomas is wearing a scarf, coat, and gloves (*Thomas porte une écharpe, un manteau et des gants*). _____

3. Marie is wearing a bikini (*Marie porte un bikini*). _____

4. Eddy is using an umbrella (*Eddy utilise un parapluie*). _____

5. Sally is wearing sunglasses and sunscreen (*Sally porte des lunettes de soleil et de la crème solaire*). _____

**B. Read the following French descriptions of different weather. Circle the most appropriate clothing to wear in these different climates.**

1. Il fait froid et il neige.

| A. a coat (un manteau) | B. sandals (des sandales) | C. a swimsuit (un maillot) |
|---|---|---|

2. Il fait beau. Il fait chaud et ensoleillé.

| A. shorts (short) | B. an umbrella (un parapluie) | C. a scarf (une écharpe) |
|---|---|---|

3. Il fait mauvais. Il pleut. Il y a du vent, du tonnerre et des éclairs.

| A. an umbrella (un parapluie) | B. a swimsuit (un maillot) | C. a short skirt (une jupe courte) |
|---|---|---|

# 8.3   Present Tense of *Vouloir*

Sometimes it's essential to indicate if there's something you want or if you have a strong will for something. That's where the verb *vouloir* comes in. It means 'to want'.

| Vouloir *to want* | | | |
|---|---|---|---|
| je | **veux** | nous | **voulons** |
| tu | **veux** | vous | **voulez** |
| il | | ils | |
| elle | **veut** | elles | **veulent** |

More important verbs

Speak Abroad
Academy

Here's how it's used:

| | | |
|---|---|---|
| **I want a cat.** | → | Je veux un chat. |
| **The little girl wants a dog.** | → | La petite fille veut un chien. |
| **He wants a croissant.** | → | Il veut un croissant. |
| **She wants to go to the park.** | → | Elle veut aller au parc. |
| **We want a new car.** | → | Nous voulons une nouvelle voiture. |
| **They want a bigger house** (co-ed.). | → | Ils veulent une maison plus grande. |

## Practice 8.3 Vouloir

**Let's practice using the present tense of *vouloir*. Add the correct conjugations to the following sentences.**

1. _____ une nouvelle petite amie. (*You want a new girlfriend – inf.*)
2. _____ aller au musée aujourd'hui. (*I want to go to the museum today.*)
3. _____ faire du shopping. (*She wants to go shopping.*)
4. _____ un jardin plus grand. (*They want a bigger garden – f.*)
5. _____ un hamster. (*We want a hamster.*)
6. _____ avoir plus d'enfants. (*They want to have more children – co-ed.*)

## Politeness

In English, it would be considered rude to say 'I want juice' or 'I want coffee' if you go to a restaurant. It's just as off-putting in French. This is why it's best to not use *vouloir*, when you're in these situations. Instead, you should use the…

## 8.4 Conditional Tense of *Vouloir*

When something is in the conditional tense, it means that the verb's action is not being as strongly conveyed. It sounds a bit more uncertain. In English, this becomes 'would like' instead of 'want'. Saying you 'would like' something is a lot more polite than simply saying you want something.

| Vouloir *would want / would like* | | | |
|---|---|---|---|
| je | **voudrais** | nous | **voudrions** |
| tu | **voudrais** | vous | **voudriez** |
| il | **voudrait** | ils | **voudraient** |
| elle | | elles | |

With this conditional tense, it becomes way more polite to ask for things that you want. For example:

| | | |
|---|---|---|
| **I would like a newspaper.** | → | Je voudrais un journal. |
| **She would like a coffee.** | → | Elle voudrait un café. |
| **He would like a dessert.** | → | Il voudrait un dessert. |
| **We would like a bottle of wine.** | → | Nous voudrions une bouteille de vin. |
| **They would like a menu** (co-ed.). | → | Ils voudraient un menu. |

## Practice 8.4 Conditional *Vouloir*

**A. Translate the following sentences into French using what you just learned about the conditional tense of *vouloir*.**

1. He would like some flowers.

   _____

2. We would like three coffees, please.

   _____

3. I would like a blue shirt and a white skirt.

   _____

4. They would like a table (co-ed.).

   _____

5. She would like a black coat.

   _____

**B. Read the following French dialogue between a mother and her daughter. Then, refer to the glossary provided and answer the following questions.**

PAULINE : Nous avons besoin d'un cadeau pour l'anniversaire de Grand-mère.

ANNA : Elle voudrait avoir un nouveau chat.

PAULINE : Elle a quatre chats ! Cinq chats, c'est trop.

ANNA : Bon, d'accord. Elle veut une robe. Une robe rouge ! Et des chaussures blanches aussi.

PAULINE : Une robe rouge pour Mamie ?

ANNA : Oui, il y a un nouveau magasin à côté de la boulangerie. Les vêtements sont si jolis !

PAULINE : Ah ! C'est toi qui veux de nouveaux vêtements. C'est ça, Anna ?

**Glossary**

| | |
|---|---|
| Nous avons besoin : we need | À côté : next to |
| Un cadeau : a gift | Les vêtements : the clothes |
| Anniversaire : birthday | C'est toi : it's you |
| Mamie : Grandma | C'est ça ? : is that right? |

1. Whose birthday is it? _____
2. What was Anna's first suggestion? _____
3. Where is the new store located? _____

**C. Translate the following French sentences into English using everything you've learned so far.**

1. Nous faisons nos courses au supermarché. Les fruits sont chers !
   _____

2. Il fait beau. Il y a des fleurs dans le parc. Je veux aller au parc.
   _____

3. Il fait le lit. Tu fais la vaisselle. Et moi ? Je suis dans un bar avec des amis.
   _____

4. Il pleut. Les nouveaux vêtements sont mouillés.
   _____

5. Il fait froid aujourd'hui ! Je voudrais un café chaud. Elle veut aussi du café.
   _____

## 8.5   Present Tense of *Porter*

We've used this verb in some exercises in this chapter. *Porter* means 'to wear' or 'to carry'. It's most commonly used to indicate what clothes you're wearing.

| Porter *to wear / to carry* | | | |
|---|---|---|---|
| je | **porte** | nous | **portons** |
| tu | **portes** | vous | **portez** |
| il | **porte** | ils | **portent** |
| elle | | elles | |

Here's how it's used in different sentences...

| | | |
|---|---|---|
| **I'm wearing an expensive necklace.** | → | Je porte un collier cher. |
| **He's wearing an ugly jacket.** | → | Il porte une veste moche. |
| **She's carrying a heavy bag.** | → | Elle porte un sac lourd. |
| **We're wearing formal clothes.** | → | Nous portons des vêtements formels. |

You get the idea! Now, it's time to test your knowledge!

## Practice 8.5 *Porter*

**A. Fill in the blanks with the correct conjugation for each sentence.**

1. _____ chaussures chères. (*He's wearing expensive shoes.*)
2. _____ une belle écharpe. (*You're wearing a beautiful scarf – inf.*)
3. _____ la même robe. (*They're wearing the same dress – f.*)
4. _____ des lunettes de soleil dehors. (*She wears sunglasses outside.*)
5. _____ vêtements tous les jours. (*I wear clothes every day.*)
6. _____ robes moches. (*We are wearing ugly dresses.*)
7. _____ chapeaux roses (*They're wearing pink hats – co-ed.*)

**B. Translate the following sentences into English using everything you've learned so far.**

1. C'est une belle journée. Je porte une nouvelle chemise et nous allons dans un restaurant cher.

   _____

2. Je porte une veste marron, mais je voudrais une veste noire.

   _____

3. Il fait chaud aujourd'hui. Je porte des lunettes de soleil et un short. Je vais au parc avec des amis.

   _____

4. Elle porte des vêtements chers, mais ces vêtements sont vieux et moches.

   _____

5. Je voudrais quatre petits chapeaux jaunes, s'il vous plaît. Ils sont pour mes chats !

   _____

## CHAPTER 9:
# EATING AND DRINKING
*I EAT THE CHEESE, YOU DRINK THE WINE*

## 9.1 Food & Drink Vocabulary

With all the hard work you've done, you deserve to be rewarded! Therefore, it's time for a fun chapter: food and drink! We've covered some French words for food and drink already, but you can never learn enough words when it comes to eating and drinking. Here are some important words to keep in mind:

| English | French | Pronunciation |
|---------|--------|---------------|
| Bread | **pain (m.)** | [pahn] |
| Cheese | **fromage (m.)** | [froh-mahj] |
| Ham | **jambon (m.)** | [jahm-boh~] |
| Sausages | **saucisses (f.)** | [soh-sees] |
| Egg | **œuf (m.)** | [øf] |
| Sugar | **sucre (m.)** | [suh-krə] |
| Butter | **beurre (m.)** | [bør] |
| Fish | **poisson (m.)** | [pwah-soh~] |
| Beef | **bœuf (m.)** | [bøf] |
| Chicken | **poulet (m.)** | [poo-lay] |
| Vegetables | **légumes (m.)** | [lay-guhm] |
| Meat | **viande (f.)** | [vee-ah~-də] |
| Salad | **salade (f.)** | [sah-lahd] |
| Mushroom | **champignon (m.)** | [shohm-peen-yoh~] |
| Potato | **pomme de terre (f.)** | [pohm də tayr] |
| Chocolate | **chocolat (m.)** | [shoh-koh-lah] |
| Ice Cream | **glace (f.)** | [glahss] |
| Cake | **gâteau (m.)** | [gah-toh] |

Speak Abroad
Academy

| Wine | **vin (m.)** | *[vahn]* |
| Water | **eau (f.)** | *[oh]* |
| Milk | **lait (m.)** | *[lay]* |
| Beer | **bière (f.)** | *[beey-ayr]* |
| Juice | **jus (m.)** | *[juh]* |
| Coffee | **café (m.)** | *[kah-fay]* |
| Tea | **thé (m.)** | *[tay]* |
| Hot Chocolate | **chocolat chaud (m.)** | *[shoh-koh-lah shoh]* |
| | | |
| Fruit | **fruit (m.)** | *[frwee]* |
| Apple | **pomme (f.)** | *[pohm]* |
| Orange | **orange (f.)** | *[ohr-ah~-jə]* |
| Banana | **banane (f.)** | *[bah-nahn]* |
| Pear | **poire (f.)** | *[pwahr]* |
| Cherry | **cerise (f.)** | *[sə-reez]* |
| Strawberry | **fraise (f.)** | *[frayz]* |
| Lemon | **citron (m.)** | *[seet-roh~]* |
| Peach | **pêche (f.)** | *[paysh]* |
| | | |
| Meal | **repas (m.)** | *[rə-pah]* |
| Breakfast | **petit-déjeuner (m.)** | *[pə-tee day-jø-nay]* |
| Lunch | **déjeuner (m.)** | *[day-jø-nay]* |
| Dinner | **dîner (m.)** | *[dee-nay]* |
| Dessert | **dessert (m.)** | *[day-sayr]* |

You know all fun experiences are incomplete without some practice so here it is! Time for you to challenge yourself:

## Practice 9.1 Food

### A. Can you remember what these foods are in English?

1. Une salade _____
2. Du pain et du fromage _____
3. Une bière _____
4. Du poisson et des légumes _____
5. Un café avec du sucre _____
6. Une pomme _____
7. Poulet et bœuf _____
8. Un thé avec du lait _____

### B. Using what you know about numbers, see if you can identify what these plural food items are.

1. Dix œufs _____
2. Cinq pommes _____
3. Quinze pommes de terre _____
4. Trois bananes _____
5. Trente-cinq citrons _____
6. Dix-neuf champignons _____
7. Deux bières _____
8. Vingt pêches _____

### C. Translate the following sentences into French using the conditional form of *vouloir*.

1. I would like a coffee with milk and sugar.

   _____

2. I would like a salad.

   _____

3. We would like meat and vegetables.

   _____

4. He would like a beer and she would like a juice.

   _____

5. She would like mushrooms in the salad.

   _____

6. They would like bread and butter (co-ed.).

   _____

**D. Translate these French sentences into English.**

1. Elle voudrait de la glace sur le gâteau.

   _____

2. Il voudrait du poisson et des légumes pour le dîner.

   _____

3. Je voudrais une bière avec le dîner.

   _____

4. Nous voudrions de la glace pour le dessert.

   _____

5. Je voudrais des fraises et du chocolat.

   _____

6. Ils voudraient des œufs, du jambon et du pain.

   _____

# 9.2 Conveying Units of Food & Drink

Sometimes it's necessary to describe whether you want a cup of coffee or a pot of coffee. The following words will help you do that:

| English | French | Pronunciation |
|---------|--------|---------------|
| A cup of... | **une tasse de** | [uhn tahs də] |
| A bottle of... | **une bouteille de** | [uhn boo-tay də] |
| A glass of... | **un verre de** | [ahn vayr də] |
| A bowl of... | **un bol de** | [ahn bohl də] |
| A plate of... | **une assiette de** | [uhn plah də] |
| A spoonful of... | **une cuillerée de** | [uhn kwee-yə-ray də] |
| A handful of... | **une poignée de** | [uhn pwahn-yay də] |

Time for a practice test once again!

## Practice 9.2 Units of Food

**A. Translate the following French sentences into English using what we've learned so far in this chapter.**

1. Une cuillerée de sucre _____

2. Une tasse de lait _____

3. Deux tasses de lait _____

4.  Une poignée de fraises _____

5.  Une assiette de saucisses _____

6.  Un verre de vin _____

7.  Une bouteille de vin _____

8.  Un bol de cerises _____

**B. Let's make the sentences a little more complex.**

1.  Il y a une tasse de café sur la table.

    _____

2.  Il y a une assiette d'œufs et de jambon dans la cuisine.

    _____

3.  Il y a du thé dans la tasse, mais je voudrais un café.

    _____

4.  Il y a cinq bouteilles de bière sur la table dans le jardin.

    _____

5.  Il y a une bouteille de vin dans la chambre. C'est pour toi et moi.

    _____

# 9.3 Present Tense of *Manger*

Now that you know the French words for various foods and drinks, it's time to introduce the most important verb in this topic. It's the verb *manger*! As I'm sure you can guess, it means 'to eat' and it's extremely useful in everyday life.

| Manger *to eat* | | | |
|---|---|---|---|
| je | **mange** | nous | **mangeons** |
| tu | **manges** | vous | **mangez** |
| il | **mange** | ils | **mangent** |
| elle | | elles | |

Here's how it's used in a sentence…

| **Every day, I eat a big lunch.** | → | Chaque jour, je mange un gros déjeuner. |
| **He eats a lot.** | → | Il mange beaucoup. |
| **She eats dessert every evening.** | → | Elle mange du dessert chaque soir. |

Eating and drinking

| **We are eating eggs and sausages for breakfast.** | → | Nous mangeons des œufs et des saucisses au petit déjeuner. |
| **You eat like a cow** (inf.). | → | Tu manges comme une vache. |
| **They are eating together** (co-ed.). | → | Ils mangent ensemble. |

Have you noticed that 'I eat' and 'they are eating' are both translated by the present tense of 'manger'? Actually, French people use the present tense for activities that take place regularly and actions that are happening right now. It makes things so much easier when you think about it!

Let's do a practice exercise to really solidify that knowledge! Are you with me?

## Practice 9.3 *Manger*

**A. Fill the blanks with the correct conjugations of *manger*.**

1. _____ au restaurant. (*They are eating at the restaurant* – f.)
2. _____ trop bruyamment. (*You are eating too loudly* – inf.)
3. _____ parce que j'ai faim. (*I'm eating because I'm hungry.*)
4. _____ tout le gâteau. (*They are eating all the cake* – co-ed.)
5. _____ encore une salade. (*She is eating a salad again.*)
6. _____ une grande assiette de légumes. (*He is eating a big plate of vegetables.*)
7. _____ avec moi ce soir. (*You are eating with me tonight* – form.)
8. _____ trop de glace. (*We are eating too much ice cream.*)

**B. Write the following sentences in French.**

1. I'm eating an apple for breakfast.

   _____

2. Michael and Marie are eating together.

   _____

3. We are eating a big plate of fish. It's delicious!

   _____

4. They (co-ed.) are eating in the garden tonight.

   _____

5. You (*inf.*) are eating outside with the cow tonight.

   _____

6. She's eating a handful of strawberries.

_____

7. He is eating ice cream for dessert.

_____

# 9.4  Present Tense of *Boire*

You know how to say 'to eat,' but how about 'to drink'? That's where *boire* comes in!

| Boire *to drink* | | | |
|---|---|---|---|
| je | **bois** | nous | **buvons** |
| tu | **bois** | vous | **buvez** |
| il | **boit** | ils | **boivent** |
| elle | | elles | |

Here's how it's used in a sentence…

| | | |
|---|---|---|
| **I drink too much beer.** | → | Je bois trop de bière. |
| **He's drinking a glass of orange juice.** | → | Il boit un verre de jus d'orange. |
| **She's drinking a bottle of water.** | → | Elle boit une bouteille d'eau. |
| **You drink a lot of juice** (inf.). | → | Tu bois beaucoup de jus. |
| **We are drinking champagne in the morning.** | → | Nous buvons du champagne le matin. |
| **They are drinking wine at the restaurant** (co-ed.). | → | Ils boivent du vin au restaurant. |
| **They are drinking wine at the bar** (f.). | → | Elles boivent du vin au bar. |

Now you have the perfect companion for *manger*!

## Practice 9.4 *Boire*

**A. Let's put your expanded French vocabulary to the test. Translate the following French sentences into English.**

1. Chaque soir, il boit trop de bière et je mange trop de gâteau.

_____

2. Nous sommes au restaurant. Il y a une grande assiette de bœuf sur la table. C'est délicieux !

_____

3. Pour le petit-déjeuner, je bois du café avec du sucre et du lait. Louis boit un verre de jus de pomme.

_____

4. Il y a une assiette d'œufs et de saucisses dans la cuisine. C'est pour toi !

_____

5. Andy et Angela boivent beaucoup de vin. Bob et moi, nous mangeons beaucoup de salade.

_____

**B. Time for a reading comprehension exercise. Read the following passage and answer the questions by referring to the glossary.**

*Au restaurant*

Nous sommes dans un restaurant français populaire. Nous sommes huit à la table. Nous travaillons ensemble dans le même bureau. La table est très grande. Nous commandons quatre bouteilles de vin et beaucoup de viande. Je mange du bœuf et je bois un verre de vin. Il y a aussi du poulet, du poisson et des légumes. C'est délicieux ! Toute la soirée, nous parlons, rions, mangeons et buvons. Quelle merveilleuse soirée !

**Glossary**

| | |
|---|---|
| Populaire : popular | Toute la soirée : all night |
| Nous travaillons ensemble : we work together | Nous parlons : we talk |
| Même : same | Nous rions : we laugh |
| Nous commandons : we order | Merveilleuse : marvellous |

1. What type of restaurant are they eating at? _____
2. How many people are at the table? _____
3. What's the relationship between all the people at dinner?

   _____
4. What do they order to drink? _____
5. Name all the food items that they order for dinner.

   _____

CHAPTER 10:

# LIKES AND DISLIKES
## I LIKE LEARNING FRENCH

## 10.1   The Present Tense of *Aimer*

Now, we can finally start expressing our opinions. With the verb *Aimer,* which means 'to like' or 'to love', you can let others know about all the things that you enjoy. This verb will come in handy when you're getting to know people.

| Aimer *to like / to love* | | | |
|---|---|---|---|
| j' | **aime** | nous | **aimons** |
| tu | **aimes** | vous | **aimez** |
| il | **aime** | ils | **aiment** |
| elle | | elles | |

Here's how it's used in a sentence…

| | | |
|---|---|---|
| **I like cows.** | → | J'aime les vaches. |
| **He likes the color pink.** | → | Il aime la couleur rose. |
| **She likes her new house.** | → | Elle aime sa nouvelle maison. |
| **We like the French restaurant.** | → | Nous aimons le restaurant français. |
| **You like this car a lot** (form.). | → | Vous aimez beaucoup cette voiture. |
| **You like France** (inf.). | → | Tu aimes la France. |
| **They like the blue sofa** (co-ed.). | → | Ils aiment le sofa bleu. |

> **Tip:** Remember that when you're using *aimer* to talk about yourself, **je** becomes **j'** because the next word begins with a vowel. It's always **j'aime** and never, ever *je aime*!

Let's check your comprehension by introducing a small practice exercise! Are you ready?

## Practice 10.1 *Aimer*

**A. Fill in the blanks with the correct form of *aimer* for these simple sentences.**

1. Tu _____ les chats.
2. J'_____ le fromage français.
3. Nous _____ les fleurs jaunes.
4. Vous _____ le grand jardin.
5. Il _____ la belle femme.
6. Elle _____ la nouvelle boutique.
7. Ils _____ la voiture chère.
8. Elles _____ la glace.

# 10.2 Hobbies & Interests Vocabulary

In order to practice using *aimer*, it's helpful to know the French words for common interests and hobbies. Which of the following do you like and enjoy? Can you say it in French using what you just learned about *aimer*?

| English | French | Pronunciation |
|---|---|---|
| Music | **la musique (f.)** | *[lah muh-zeek]* |
| Computer Games | **les jeux sur ordinateur (m.)** | *[lay jə suhr ohr-dee-nah-tør]* |
| Video Games | **les jeux vidéo (m.)** | *[lay jə vee-day-oh]* |
| Board Games | **les jeux de société (m.)** | *[lay jə də sohs-yay-tay]* |
| Photography | **la photographie (f.)** | *[lah foh-toh-grah-fee]* |
| Books | **les livres (m.)** | *[lay lee-vrə]* |
| Fiction Novels | **les romans de fiction (m.)** | *[lay roh-mah~ də feeks-yoh~]* |
| Poetry | **la poésie (f.)** | *[lah poh-ay-zee]* |
| Movies | **les films (m.)** | *[lay feelm]* |
| Art | **l'art (m.)** | *[lahr]* |
| Chess | **les échecs (m.)** | *[lay zay-shayk]* |
| Sports | **le sport (m.)** | *[lay spohr]* |
| Basketball | **le basketball (m.)** | *[lə basketball]* |
| Soccer | **le football (m.)** | *[lə football]* |
| Tennis | **le tennis (m.)** | *[lə tennis]* |

## Practice 10.2 Hobbies

**A. Using what you learned above, write the following sentences in French.**

1.  Julia likes poetry. _____
2.  We like music a lot. _____
3.  I like fiction novels. _____
4.  They (co-ed.) like photography. _____
5.  He likes board games. _____
6.  You like art a lot. _____

## Additional Verbs

Occasionally, you might wish to express the actions involved in pursuing your hobbies. The table below introduces various verbs commonly associated with the aforementioned hobbies (poetry, music, board games) or can be used independently.

| English | French | Pronunciation |
|---|---|---|
| To listen to | **écouter** | [ay-kooh-tay] |
| To play | **jouer** | [joo-ay] |
| To write | **écrire** | [ayk-reer] |
| To watch | **regarder** | [rə-gahr-day] |
| To read | **lire** | [leer] |
| To cook | **cuisiner** | [kwee-zee-nay] |
| To draw | **dessiner** | [day-see-nay] |
| To dance | **danser** | [dah~-say] |
| To paint | **peindre** | [pahn-drə] |

Here are some examples of how to use the above verbs with the new vocabulary you've learned so far.

**I like to listen to music.** → J'aime écouter de la musique.

**She likes to play video games.** → Elle aime jouer aux jeux vidéo.

**He likes to play basketball.** → Il aime jouer au basketball.

**We like to write novels.** → Nous aimons écrire des romans.

Speak Abroad
Academy

| You like to watch TV (form.). | → | Vous aimez regarder la télévision. |
| You like to read (inf.). | → | Tu aimes lire. |
| They like to cook (co-ed.). | → | Ils aiment cuisiner. |
| They like to dance together (f.). | → | Elles aiment danser ensemble. |

> **Tip:** Keep in mind that whenever a verb immediately follows another verb (e.g. 'to like to cook' where 'to like' and 'to cook' are both verbs), it doesn't follow the same conjugation. For example, if you want to say 'I like to go...' you would say **'J'aime aller...'** *not* 'J'aime vais.'

## 10.3  Using *Faire* with Hobbies

We learned *faire* which means 'to do' or 'to make' in an earlier chapter. It comes in handy when you're talking about certain hobbies. For example:

| English | French | Pronunciation |
| --- | --- | --- |
| Baking | **(faire de) la pâtisserie (f.)** | *[pə'tiːsərɪ]* |
| Hiking | **(faire de) la randonnée (f.)** | *[roh~-doh-nay]* |
| Biking/ cycling | **(faire du) cyclisme (m.)** | *[seek-leezm]* |
| Gardening | **(faire du) jardinage (m.)** | *[jahr-dee-nahj]* |
| Exercising/ working out | **(faire de) l'entraînement (m.)** | *[oh~-tray-nə-moh~]* |
| Sailing | **(faire de) la voile (f.)** | *[vɔɪl]* |
| Shopping | **(faire du) shopping (m.)** | *[shopping]* |

Attempt the following practice exercise to really solidify your understanding.

### Practice 10.3 *Faire* + hobbies

#### A. Write the following sentences in French.

1. He likes to play chess. _____
2. We like to dance in the kitchen. _____
3. She likes to bake. _____

4.  They (co-ed.) like to play video games. _____
    _____

5.  I like to play board games. _____

6.  You (inf.) like to listen to music and I like to dance. _____
    _____

**B. Translate the following sentences into English.**

1.  Ils aiment s'entraîner ensemble dans le jardin.
    _____

2.  Elle aime faire du sport à l'école.
    _____

3.  Nous aimons écouter de la musique le matin.
    _____

4.  Il aime manger des gâteaux. J'aime faire des gâteaux.
    _____

5.  J'aime regarder la télévision avec mon ami.
    _____

6.  Elles aiment faire du shopping à Paris.
    _____

7.  Tu aimes faire du jardinage.
    _____

8.  Vous aimez lire des livres intéressants.
    _____

**C. Let's make these sentences more complex and combine everything we've learned so far. Translate these sentences into English.**

1.  Il a une télévision parce qu'il aime les films.
    _____

2.  Rachel aime la viande. Elle voudrait une assiette de poulet, s'il vous plaît.
    _____

3.  J'aime jouer au foot avec le chien blanc.
    _____

4.  Nous aimons jouer aux jeux vidéo avec de belles femmes.
    _____

5.  Elles aiment jouer aux échecs dans le jardin.
    _____

6.  Elles aiment les fleurs. Tous les jours, ils aiment jardiner ensemble.
    _____

Speak Abroad
Academy

## 10.4   Expressing Your Dislikes

For the first time in this book, we'll begin constructing a negative sentence. Using the same verb, *aimer*, and the same conjugations, you can also express that you don't like something. The following affirmative sentences become negative sentences like this...

| | | |
|---|---|---|
| **I don't like to listen to music.** | → | Je n'aime pas écouter de la musique. |
| **She doesn't like to play video games.** | → | Elle n'aime pas jouer aux jeux vidéo. |
| **He doesn't like to play basketball.** | → | Il n'aime pas jouer au basketball. |
| **We don't like to write novels.** | → | Nous n'aimons pas écrire des romans. |
| **You don't like to watch TV** (form.). | → | Vous n'aimez pas regarder la télévision. |
| **You don't like to read** (inf.). | → | Tu n'aimes pas lire. |
| **They don't like to cook** (co-ed.). | → | Ils n'aiment pas cuisiner. |
| **They don't like to dance together** (f.). | → | Elles n'aiment pas danser ensemble. |

> **Tip:** In order to use *aimer* in a negative sentence, you add **n'** in front of the *aimer* conjugation and then add **pas** after it. Since **n** is a consonant and not a vowel, this also means that **j'** turns back into **je**. So **j'aime** becomes **je n'aime pas**.

Try the following practice exercise to really solidify your understanding.

### Practice 10.4 Dislikes

**A. Let's get used to saying you 'don't like' something with** *aimer.* **Turn these affirmative sentences from an earlier exercise into negative sentences.**

1. _____ chats. (*You don't like cats – inf.*)
2. _____ fromage français.(*I don't like French cheese.*)
3. _____ fleurs jaunes.(*We don't like yellow flowers.*)

4. _____ le grand jardin. (*You don't like the big garden – form.*)
5. _____ la belle femme. (*He doesn't like the beautiful woman.*)
6. _____ la nouvelle boutique. (*She doesn't like the new shop.*)
7. _____ la voiture chère. (*They don't like the expensive car – co-ed.*)
8. _____ la glace. (*They don't like ice cream – f.*)

## B. Turn the following affirmative sentences into negative sentences.

1. J'aime les musées. _____
2. Elle aime les chats noirs. _____
3. Nous aimons le vin. _____
4. Ils aiment manger dans des restaurants chers. _____
   _____
5. Vous aimez regarder la télévision. _____
   _____
6. Ils aiment manger de la glace. _____
7. Vous aimez jouer au tennis. _____
8. Il aime lire dans le jardin. _____

## C. Turn the following negative sentences into affirmative sentences.

1. Ils n'aiment pas cuisiner. _____
2. Il n'aime pas porter des chaussures. _____
3. Je n'aime pas danser. _____
4. Elle n'aime pas boire de la bière. _____
5. Vous n'aimez pas les vaches. _____
6. Ils n'aiment pas manger du fromage. _____
7. Nous n'aimons pas regarder la télévision le soir. _____
   _____
8. Tu n'aimes pas le nouveau chat. _____

**D. Translate the following French sentences into English.**

1. Nous n'aimons pas le canapé noir dans le salon.

   _____

2. Il y a trois chiens devant la maison. J'aime le chien noir.

   _____

3. Ils n'aiment pas jouer au football dans le parc.

   _____

4. Le jeune homme aime faire du vélo. Il est très rapide.

   _____

5. Je suis très heureux. Il y a vingt livres sur la table. J'aime lire.

   _____

6. Elle aime jouer au basket, mais je n'aime pas le sport. J'aime jouer aux échecs.

   _____

**E. Translate these English sentences into French.**

1. He wants a big garden. He likes to garden.

   _____

2. She eats a lot, but she doesn't like vegetables.

   _____

3. I like the color yellow. I don't like the color black.

   _____

4. You *(inf.)* like the rich woman. I like the loyal man.

   _____

5. We like the bread at the bakery. We don't like the bread at the restaurant.

   _____

6. They don't like to watch TV together.

   _____

## CHAPTER 11:
# NEGATION
*I DON'T DANCE*

## 11.1 Constructing Negative Sentences with *Ne... pas*

In the previous chapter, you learned how to construct a negative French sentence by saying you 'do not like' something. As you know, this is not the only type of negative sentence that exists. In fact, every single verb can be used negatively. For example, you can say 'I go' and 'I don't go' or 'I have' and 'I don't have'.

An affirmative sentence would be 'the cat is blue'. In retort to this, a negative sentence would be 'the cat is not blue'.

To make a sentence negative, you add the words **ne... pas**, with the verb in the sentence. If the verb begins with a vowel, it becomes **n'... pas.** This is the equivalent of adding 'do not' to a sentence.

Here are some examples:

| | | |
|---|---|---|
| **I like cats.** | → | **I don't like cats.** |
| J'aime les chats. | → | Je n'aime pas les chats. |
| **I am a cat.** | → | **I'm not a cat.** |
| Je suis un chat. | → | Je ne suis pas un chat. |
| **I'm going to the church.** | → | **I'm not going to the church.** |
| Je vais à l'église. | → | Je ne vais pas à l'église. |
| **You are happy** (inf.). | → | **You are not happy.** |
| Tu es heureux. | → | Tu n'es pas heureux. |
| **We want a new car.** | → | **We don't want a new car.** |
| Nous voulons une nouvelle voiture. | → | Nous ne voulons pas de nouvelle voiture. |
| **They have a daughter** (co-ed.). | → | **They don't have a daughter.** |
| Ils ont une fille. | → | Ils n'ont pas de fille. |

It's important to know that when there's an indefinite article (un/une) or a partitive article (du/de la/des) used to mean 'some' after a negative, the article can often change to 'de' or 'd'.

**She eats meat.** → **She doesn't eat meat.**

Elle mange de la viande. → Elle ne mange pas de viande.

**He drinks beer.** → **He does not drink beer.**

Il boit de la bière. → Il ne boit pas de bière.

**He has some new books.** → **He does not have any new books.**

Il a des nouveaux livres. → Il n'a pas de nouveaux livres.

## Practice 11.1 *Ne... pas*

**A. Let's practice turning affirmative sentences into negative sentences. For now, let's stick to the first-person singular pronoun.**

1. Je suis une vache. _____

2. Je mange un gâteau. _____

3. Je vais à la gare. _____

4. J'ai un gentil frère. _____

5. Je veux un nouveau chat. _____

6. Je voudrais un bol de cerises. _____

7. Je porte un chapeau bleu. _____

8. J'aime les fleurs. _____

9. Je bois un verre de vin. _____

**B. Now, let's bring in the other subject pronouns. Turn these following sentences into negative sentences.**

1. Vous aimez le parapluie jaune. _____

2. Il veut un verre d'eau. _____

3. Elle va sortir. _____

4. Elles portent de nouveaux vêtements. _____

5. Nous buvons beaucoup de jus d'orange. _____

6. Ils sont des hommes riches. _____

7. Elle est triste. _____

8. Nous avons deux fils. _____

9. Vous allez à l'école. _____

## C. Write the following negative sentences in French.

1. She doesn't want the small house. _____

2. I don't want to read a book. _____

3. We don't eat meat. _____

4. They *(co-ed.)* don't have a white cat. _____

5. I am not a doctor. _____

6. He doesn't eat fish. _____

7. You *(inf.)* are not going outside. _____

## D. Which of the following negative sentences are grammatically incorrect?

1. _____ Je mange pas de viande.

2. _____ Je ne sors pas de la maison.

3. _____ Je ne suis pas content.

4. _____ Nous ne voulons sortir.

5. _____ Vous n'aimez pas l'école.

6. _____ Ils sont pas grands.

## E. Correct the incorrect sentences in the prior exercise.

1. _____

2. _____

3. _____

# 11.2 Constructing Negative Sentences with Ne... jamais

Sometimes it isn't enough to say you aren't doing something; sometimes it's necessary to say you *never* do something. That's where **ne... jamais** comes in. This indicates that the verb is never performed.

| | | |
|---|---|---|
| **She never listens.** | → | Elle n'écoute jamais. |
| **I never go outside.** | → | Je ne sors jamais. |
| **He never eats vegetables.** | → | Il ne mange jamais de légumes. |

**They never have money.** *(co-ed.)* → Ils n'ont jamais d'argent.

**We never drink orange juice.** → Nous ne buvons jamais de jus d'orange.

You get the idea!

## Practice 11.2 Ne... jamais

**A. Turn these affirmative sentences into negative sentences using ne... jamais.**

1. Elle a de l'argent._____

2. Le grand homme va au supermarché. _____

3. Je mange de la viande. _____

4. Nous allons à l'école. _____

5. Ils prennent le petit-déjeuner ensemble. _____

6. Vous buvez de la bière. _____

7. Elles font le lit. _____

8. Tu vas à l'église. _____

**B. Which of the following negative sentences are grammatically incorrect?**

1. Il travaille jamais.

2. Elle ne m'écoute jamais.

3. Je ne sors de l'école.

4. Nous ne mangeons jamais tard.

5. Vous ne aimez pas aller avec moi.

6. Tu ne vas jamais au théâtre.

**C. Correct the incorrect sentences in the prior exercise.**

1. _____

2. _____

3. _____

**D. Read the following short French passage and answer the questions using the glossary provided. Can you understand what the speaker is complaining about?**

Mon fils a deux ans. Ce n'est pas un garçon calme, il est bruyant. Il ne mange jamais ses légumes et il ne range jamais ses affaires. Nous n'allons jamais au restaurant, parce qu'il est très vilain. Je suis fatigué. J'ai besoin de vacances !

**Glossary:**

Garçon calme : quiet boy

Bruyant : noisy

Toujours : always

Ranger ses affaires : tidy up his things

Vilain : naughty

Fatigué : tired

J'ai besoin : I need

Vacances : a vacation

1. How old is the speaker's son? _____
2. Is the son quiet or noisy? _____
3. What does he never eat? _____
4. Where does the speaker never take his son? _____
5. What does the speaker need? _____

**E. Translate the following French sentences into English.**

1. Elle n'aime pas manger de dessert. Elle mange des salades.

   _____

2. J'ai cinq enfants ; je ne vais jamais au cinéma !

   _____

3. Il aime aller dans des restaurants chers, mais il n'a jamais d'argent.

   _____

4. Tu aimes la poésie triste. Tu n'es jamais heureux !

   _____

5. Nous ne buvons jamais de bière. Nous voudrions avoir deux verres de vin. _____

Speak Abroad
Academy

CHAPTER 12:

# ASKING QUESTIONS

*DO YOU LIKE FRENCH?*

## 12.1   Asking Questions with *Est-ce que...*

So far, you've practiced making a lot of statements. But what about asking questions? Just like English, there are many ways to ask questions in French. It all depends on what type of information you're looking for.

The most basic way to ask a question is by beginning a sentence with **est-ce que...** (pronounced 'ess keu') This can turn any statement into a yes or no question. It translates to 'is it that..?' which is understood more commonly in English as 'is it so that..?'

> **Tip: *Est-ce que*** becomes ***est-ce qu'*** in front of a vowel: **Do they?** →
> **Est-ce qu'ils ?**

Let's see how this works!

**You like apples.**               →    **Do you like apples?**

Tu aimes les pommes.        →    Est-ce que tu aimes les pommes ?

**She has a big house.**          →    **Does she have a big house?**

Elle a une grande maison.   →    Est-ce qu'elle a une grande maison ?

**He is going to the office.**   →    **Is he going to the office?**

Il va au bureau.                       →    Est-ce qu'il va au bureau ?

**They want to go to the museum.**   →   **Do they want to go
to the museum?**

Ils veulent aller au musée.               →   Est-ce qu'ils veulent
aller au musée ?

**I am a cow.**          →   **Am I a cow?**

Je suis une vache.   →   Est-ce que je suis une vache ?

The following practice exercise will help you test your understanding.

## Practice 12.1 *Est-ce que*

**A. Turn the following statements into questions using *est-ce que* following the examples listed above.**

1. Il a six chats. _____
2. Nous aimons la voiture orange. _____
3. Elle va à la gare. _____
4. Ils sont jeunes. _____
5. Nous avons une belle voiture. _____
6. Jenny a plus d'argent que James. _____

**B. The following statements are answers to specific questions. Write the French questions that they are answering.**

**Example:** Oui, il est prêt. Est-ce qu'il est prêt ?

1. Non, je n'aime pas les chiens. _____
2. Oui, c'est un vieil homme. _____
3. Oui, ils vont au restaurant français. _____
4. Non, nous ne sommes pas riches. _____
5. Oui, j'ai une grande maison. _____
6. Non, ils ne vont pas aller à la boulangerie. _____

# 12.2   Asking Questions with Inversions

Inverted questions tend to be more common, specifically in more formal situations. When a question is inverted, the verb goes before the subject pronoun and it's connected by a hyphen. Like this...

**Do you like apples?**   →   Aimes-tu les pommes ?
**Does she have a big house?**   →   A-t-elle une grande maison ?
**Is he going to the office?**   →   Va-t-il au bureau ?
**Do they want to go to the museum?**   →   Veulent-ils aller au musée ?
**Am I a cow?**   →   Suis-je une vache ?

Ready to practice?

**Speak Abroad**
Academy

## Practice 12.2 Inversions

**A. Turn the following statements into questions using inversions following the examples listed above.**

1.  Tu as une voiture. _____

2.  Il boit du vin. _____

3.  Nous aimons le nouveau restaurant. _____

4.  Elle fait du sport. _____

5.  Elles aiment jouer au football. _____

6.  Vous aimez lire. _____

**B. Change the following questions with *est-ce que* into inverted questions.**

1.  Est-ce que vous faites toujours du sport les week-ends ?

2.  Est-ce que je dois finir mon examen ce matin ?

3.  Est-ce qu'elle est contente de venir ici ?

4.  Est-ce que nous allons tous au même restaurant ?

5.  Est-ce qu'il va au bureau le samedi ?

6.  Est-ce que tu es content de regarder ce film avec moi ?

# 12.3   Who, What, Where...

Without English words like who, what, or where, it would be extremely difficult to ask certain questions. Of course, there are others too like when, how, and why, but for now, let's focus on these three.

In French, the equivalents of these words are:

| | | |
|---|---|---|
| who | **qui** | [kee] |
| what* | **quoi / que / quel / quelle** | [kwah] / [kə]/[quayl] / [quayl] |
| where | **où** | [oo] |

We can ask questions with them like this:

| English | French + Pronunciation | Example |
|---|---|---|
| who | **qui**<br>*[kee]* | **Who is the woman in the black dress?** → Qui est la femme avec la robe noire ?<br><br>**Who is your best friend?** → Qui est ton meilleur ami ? |
| what* | **quoi / que / quel / quelle**<br>*[kwah] / [kə]/[quayl] / [quayl]* | **What does he want?** → Que veut-il ?<br><br>**What day is it?** → Quel jour sommes-nous ? |
| where | **où**<br>*[oo]* | **Where is the new restaurant?** → Où est le nouveau restaurant ?<br><br>**Where is the cat?** → Où est le chat ? |

## *A Note on 'What'

There are a few different words that replace *'what'* in French. Not every word is appropriate for every type of sentence. Through practice you'll get used to each word and when it's best to use it.

Here's a few common examples for you:

| | | |
|---|---|---|
| **What time is it?** | → | Quelle heure est-il ? |
| **How old is she?** | → | Quel âge a-t-elle ? |
| **What is your favorite movie?** | → | Quel est ton film préféré ? |
| **What are you eating tonight?** | → | Que mangez-vous ce soir ? |

## Practice 12.3 Who, What, Where

**Answer the following questions in French using the clues given to you.**

**\*Note : *'Where is'* can be translated by Où est or Où se trouve.**

1. Où se trouve votre école ?
   _____ (est/ mon école/ l'église/ en face de)
2. Qui est l'homme au chapeau noir ?
   _____ (mon père/ c'est)
3. Quelle est ta couleur préférée ?
   _____ (le violet/ est/ ma couleur préférée)
4. Qui est ta femme ?
   _____ (est/ une écrivaine/ ma femme)
5. Où se trouve le vieux musée ?
   _____ (à côté du/ il est/ nouveau restaurant)

# 12.4   When, How, Why

Now it's time for the next set of important interrogative words! These question allies add depth and curiosity to your expressions, allowing you to navigate the intricacies of time, manner, and reason.

| when | **quand** | *[koh~]* |
| how | **comment** | *[koh-moh~]* |
| why | **pourquoi** | *[poor-kwah]* |

We can ask questions with them like this:

| | | |
|---|---|---|
| **When does she arrive?** | → | Quand arrive-t-elle ? |
| **When is the party?** | → | Quand est la fête ? |
| **How are you doing?** | → | Comment vas-tu ? |
| **How does she know?** | → | Comment le sait-elle ? |
| **Why are you sad?** | → | Pourquoi es-tu triste ? |
| **Why do you have an umbrella?** | → | Pourquoi as-tu un parapluie ? |

Attempt the following questions to test your understanding. Are you ready?

## Practice 12.4 When, How, Why

Answer the following questions in French using the clues given to you. For now, let's just focus on 'when' and 'how.'

1. Quand le concert commence-t-il ? *(il commence/ ce soir)*

   _____

2. Comment va votre mari ? *(très bien/ mon mari/ va)*

   _____

3. Quand vient-elle ? *(venir/ elle va/ ce soir)*

   _____

4. Quand est-ce que vous buvez du vin ? *(au restaurant/ français/ nous allons/ quand)*

   _____

5. Comment va ton frère ? *(ne va pas/ mon frère/ bien)*

   _____

# 12.5 Answering *Pourquoi*

In English, the word 'because' is crucial to provide a correct answer to the question 'why?' In French, there's an equivalent for this. In spoken French, it's generally expressed as **parce que**, while in written French, **car** is more common. For now, we'll concentrate on the former to emphasize improving spoken French.

Whenever the word following it begins with a vowel, it is shortened to **parce qu'** and joined to the next word.

This is how to construct a proper answer to *pourquoi*:

| | | |
|---|---|---|
| **I have an umbrella because it's raining.** | → | J'ai un parapluie parce qu'il pleut. |
| **He's eating because he's hungry.** | → | Il mange parce qu'il a faim. |
| **I'm happy because it's a good day.** | → | Je suis heureux parce que c'est une bonne journée. |
| **We are rich because we have many cows.** | → | Nous sommes riches parce que nous avons beaucoup de vaches. |
| **She wears a coat because she's cold.** | → | Elle porte un manteau parce qu'elle a froid. |
| **They are dancing because they're happy.** | → | Ils dansent parce qu'ils sont heureux. |

## Practice 12.5 Pourquoi

**Translate the following French sentences into English.**

1. J'ai un chat parce que j'aime les chats.
   _____

2. Il est dehors parce qu'il n'aime pas le chien.
   _____

3. Elle veut la voiture noire parce que la voiture blanche est moche.
   _____

4. Tu portes un short parce qu'il fait chaud et ensoleillé.
   _____

5. Nous jouons beaucoup aux échecs parce que nous sommes intelligents.
   _____

6. Tu manges cinq bols de glace parce que tu es triste.
   _____

# 12.6 Combining Common French Expressions with Prepositions

Here are some common expressions where these words are combined with prepositions to have a whole different meaning.

| English | French | Pronunciation |
|---|---|---|
| With whom? | **avec qui** | [ah-vayk kee] |
| For whom? | **pour qui** | [poor kee] |
| About whom? | **à propos de qui** | [ah proh-poh də kee] |
| To whom? | **pour qui** | [poor kee] |
| At whose place? | **chez qui** | [shay kee] |
| With what? | **avec quoi** | [ah-vayk kwah] |
| From where? | **d'où** | [doo] |
| Which one? | **lequel/ laquelle** | [lə-kayl lah-kayl] |

Here are some example sentences:

**Where do you come from?** → D'où viens-tu ?

**Which one do you like?** (talking about a shirt) → Tu préfères laquelle ?

**Who is this cow for?** → Pour qui est cette vache ?

## Practice 12.6 French Expressions with Prepositions

**A. Can you translate these French questions into English?**

1. Avec qui Jacob va-t-il au restaurant ? _____
2. Elle veut une veste ? Laquelle ? _____
3. Pour qui fais-je un gâteau ? _____
4. Chez qui es-tu ? _____
5. D'où viennent-elles ? _____
6. Avec quoi cuisinons-nous ? _____

**B. Read the following French dialogue and then answer the questions, which are written in French. Use the glossary provided for reference.**

TOM : Il y a une fête ce soir. Tu y vas ?

BEN : Oui. J'y vais avec quelqu'un.

TOM : Avec qui ?

BEN : Sasha. La femme qui travaille à la boulangerie. Et toi ?

TOM : J'y vais seul. Que vas-tu porter ?

BEN : Une chemise noire et un jean. Où est la fête ?

TOM : C'est au bar de Max.

BEN : C'est le bar avec les fleurs devant ou celui à côté de la station service ?

TOM : C'est le bar derrière l'église.

BEN : OK, à bientôt !

**Glossary:**

A party : une fête

Tonight : ce soir

Someone : quelqu'un

She works : elle travaille

Alone : seul

Gas station : station service

See you soon : à bientôt

1. Avec qui Ben va-t-il à la fête ? _____
2. Où travaille la femme ? _____
3. Que porte Ben ? _____
4. Où est le bar ? _____
5. C'est le bar de qui ? _____

## CHAPTER 13:
# TIME, DATES, AND SEASONS
*IT'S TIME TO LEARN FRENCH!*

## 13.1   Asking For & Expressing the Time

Navigating everyday life would be pretty hard without the ability to express the time. But before we can say what time it is, let's learn how to ask for the time!

There are actually many different ways to ask for the time in French. Not all of them are appropriate in every situation, since some will depend on formality. When you're around friends, family, and people you use informal language with, you can ask for the time by saying...

**Quelle heure est-il ?**

**Il est quelle heure ?**

**C'est à quelle heure ?** (*What time is it at?*) – For specific events

When you're addressing people you don't know well or anyone you use formal language with, you could ask for the time using the above questions, but you should better use...

**Puis-je avoir l'heure s'il vous plaît ?**

**Quelle heure est-il, je vous prie ?**

Yet, the most common way of asking for the time in French is...

**Quelle heure est-il ?**

Let's get those neurons firing by doing some practice exercises!

## Practice 13.1.A

**Read the following sentences. When they're not grammatically correct, mark them with an X.**

1. _____ Puis-je avoir l'heure s'il vous plaît ?
2. _____ Il heure quelle est ?
3. _____ Quelle heure est-il, je vous prie ?
4. _____ À c'est heure quelle ?

## Asking for the Time of Specific Events

Sometimes it isn't enough to just ask what time it is now. If you're waiting for a specific event, you'll also want to ask what time something takes place. You can construct these questions like this...

**What time is the party?** → À quelle heure est la fête ?
**What time is the appointment?** → À quelle heure est le rendez-vous ?
**What time is dinner?** → À quelle heure est le dîner ?

And to answer you would say...

**The party is at 20 o'clock** → La fête est à 20h.
**The appointment is at 9 o'clock** → Le rendez-vous est à 9h.
**Dinner is at 19 o'clock** → Le dîner est à 19h.

## Practice 13.1.B

**Ask for the time of the following events in French.**

1. Le film (*The movie*) _____
2. Le concert (*The concert*) _____
3. La fête d'anniversaire (*The birthday party*) _____
4. La classe des arts (*The art class*) _____
5. Le pique-nique (*The picnic*) _____

Speak Abroad
Academy

## Expressing the Time in French

Now that you know how to ask for the time, let's learn how to answer the question. The numbers you learned in an earlier chapter come in very handy here! If someone asks you what time it is and it's 2 p.m. in the afternoon, you should answer:

**Il est quatorze heures**

You may notice that the number up there is actually fourteen – not two. This is because it's customary in France to use military time. In other words, a 24-hour clock. This means that 1 p.m. becomes **treize heures**, 2 p.m. becomes **quatorze heures**, and so on.

But it is also quite common to simply say : **il est deux heures (de l'après-midi).**

If there are minutes involved, you could say : **il est quatorze heures et vingt minutes.**

But French people would most likely tell you : **il est deux heures vingt/il est quatorze heures vingt**.

## Practice 13.1.C

**Say what time it is in English using a 12-hour clock and a.m. or p.m.**

1. Il est treize heures _____
2. Il est vingt heures trente-cinq _____
3. Il est huit heures vingt _____
4. Il est vingt-trois heures quinze _____
5. Il est sept heures trente _____
6. Il est dix-huit heures et trente-trois minutes _____

## Practice 13.1.D

**State what the time is in French using the 24-hour clock.**

1. 8:20 a.m. _____
2. 10:40 a.m. _____
3. 6:10 a.m. _____
4. 3:05 p.m. _____
5. 7:50 p.m. _____
6. 11:18 p.m. _____

## Time Vocabulary

Just like in English, there are easier ways of telling the time. If it's 8:15 in the morning, you may want to say 'quarter past eight' instead of 'eight fifteen'. To simplify the expressions of time, the following words will be very useful:

| English | French | Pronunciation |
| --- | --- | --- |
| Morning | matin (m.) | [mah-tahn] |
| Afternoon | après-midi (m.) | [ahp-ray mee-dee] |
| Noon | midi (m.) | [mee-dee] |
| Evening | soir (m.) | [swahr] |
| Night | nuit (f.) | [n-wee] |
| Midnight | minuit (m.) | [meen-wee] |
| Half past... | et demi | [ay də-mee] |
| Quarter to... | moins le quart | [mwahn lə kahr] |
| Quarter past... | et quart | [ay kahr] |
| After | après | [ahp-ray] |
| Almost | presque | [praysk] |
| Hour | heure (f.) | [ør] |
| Minute | minute (f.) | [mee-nuht] |
| Second | seconde (f.) | [sə-koh~-də] |

They can be used like this:

**It's a quarter to two.** → Il est deux heures moins le quart.
**It's a quarter past two.** → Il est deux heures et quart.
**It's half past eight.** → Il est huit heures et demie.

**It's noon.** → Il est midi.
**It's almost midnight.** → Il est presque minuit.
**It's one in the morning.** → Il est une heure du matin.

> **Tip:** The official rule is that these fractions (**et quart, et demi**...) are informal and only work with a 12-hour clock. When in doubt, it's usually better to say **il est huit heures et quart** than **il est vingt heures et quart**.
>
> To clearly avoid confusion between 8 a.m. or 8 p.m. without an obvious context, you simply need to mention **'du matin'** or **'du soir'**:
>
> **He comes at 8 a.m.** → Il vient à 8 heures du matin.
> **He finishes work at 8 p.m.** → Il finit le travail à 8h du soir.

However, you might still hear fractions with a 24-hour clock when you're at the station or the airport:

**The train for Paris leaves at 13:55.** → Le train pour Paris part à 13h55 (treize heures cinquante-cinq)

## Practice 13.1.E

Using what you've learned about expressing time so far, write in French what the following times are.

1. 9:00 a.m. _____
2. 10:30 a.m. _____
3. 12:00 p.m. _____
4. 1:15 p.m. _____
5. 1:45 p.m. _____
6. 4:30 p.m. _____
7. 7:45 p.m. _____
8. 10:15 p.m. _____

# 13.2 Expressing the Date

When making plans or looking at a schedule, it's vital to know the words for the days of the weeks, the months, and other ways of measuring longer stretches of time.

| English | French | Pronunciation |
|---|---|---|
| Monday | **lundi** | *[lahn-dee]* |
| Tuesday | **mardi** | *[mahr-dee]* |
| Wednesday | **mercredi** | *[mayr-krə-dee]* |
| Thursday | **jeudi** | *[jø-dee]* |
| Friday | **vendredi** | *[voh~-drə-dee]* |
| Saturday | **samedi** | *[sah-mə-dee]* |
| Sunday | **dimanche** | *[dee-mah~-shə]* |
| | | |
| January | **janvier** | *[jah~-vee-ay]* |
| February | **février** | *[fayv-ree-yay]* |
| March | **mars** | *[mahrs]* |
| April | **avril** | *[ahv-reel]* |
| May | **mai** | *[may]* |
| June | **juin** | *[jwahn]* |
| July | **juillet** | *[jweey-ay]* |
| August | **août** | *[oot]* |
| September | **septembre** | *[sayp-tohm-brə]* |
| October | **octobre** | *[ohk-toh-brə]* |
| November | **novembre** | *[noh-vohm-brə]* |
| December | **décembre** | *[day-sohm-brə]* |
| | | |
| Yesterday | **hier** | *[eey-ayr]* |
| Today | **aujourd'hui** | *[oh-joor-dwee]* |
| Tomorrow | **demain** | *[də-mahn]* |
| Day | **jour** | *[joor]* |
| Week | **semaine** | *[sə-mayn]* |
| Month | **mois** | *[mwah]* |
| Year | **an** | *[oh~]* |
| Next... | **prochain** | *[proh-shahn]* |
| Last... | **dernier** | *[dayr-nyay]* |

**Speak Abroad**
Academy

'An' works better for a duration or a specific year:

**for 10 years** → pendant 10 ans
**in the year 2023** → en l'an 2023

But if you're talking about last year or next year, it's better to use 'année' instead:

**last year** → l'année dernière
**next year** → l'année prochaine

Here are some examples of how to express the date using these words...

**It's Monday.** → C'est lundi.
**Tomorrow is Tuesday.** → Demain c'est mardi.
**The party is next month.** → La fête est le mois prochain.
**It's July next month.** → Le prochain mois est juillet.
**She arrives in January.** → Elle arrive en janvier.
**It's Friday today.** → C'est vendredi aujourd'hui.
**Is it Saturday today?** → Est-ce que c'est samedi aujourd'hui ?
**On Monday, we eat steak.** → Le lundi, nous mangeons du steak.
**We celebrate Christmas in December.** → Nous célébrons Noël
en décembre.

## Practice 13.2.A

**Let's test your memory of the new vocabulary you've learned.**

1. October _____
2. February _____
3. June _____
4. April _____
5. August _____
6. July _____
7. Wednesday _____
8. Friday _____
9. Tuesday _____
10. Saturday _____
11. Yesterday _____
12. Tomorrow _____
13. Today _____
14. Next month _____

## Practice 13.2.B

**Write the following sentences in French.**

1. It's Thursday today. _____
2. It's November next month. _____
3. He arrives in March. _____
4. The concert is next week. _____
5. On Saturday, we go to the park. _____
6. Tomorrow is Sunday. _____

## Seasons

Let's learn the French words for the seasons. These go hand-in-hand with what you've learned about dates. Take a look at the table below and delve into the linguistic tapestry as you uncover the French vocabulary for the seasons.

| English | French | Pronunciation |
|---|---|---|
| Spring | **printemps (m.)** | *[prahn-toh~]* |
| Summer | **été (m.)** | *[ay-tay]* |
| Autumn / fall | **automne (m.)** | *[oh-tohm-nə]* |
| Winter | **hiver (m.)** | *[ee-vayr]* |

Here's how we can use these words:

| | | |
|---|---|---|
| **It's winter.** | → | C'est l'hiver. |
| **Last summer.** | → | L'été dernier. |
| **In spring, I go cycling.** | → | Au printemps, je vais faire du vélo. |
| **In summer, I like to play football.** | → | En été, j'aime jouer au football. |
| **In winter, she wears a coat.** | → | En hiver, elle porte un manteau. |
| **In autumn, we drink hot chocolate.** | → | En automne, nous buvons du chocolat chaud. |

> **Tip:** To say what day it is, what month, which season, or even which year, just add 'on est' at the beginning. It's a bit casual, but it's a lifesaver in many situations!
>
> On est lundi.
> On est en janvier.
> On est au printemps.
> On est en 2023.

Now let's do some practice exercises to really test that knowledge!

## Practice 13.2.C

**For the following months, state whether c'est l'hiver, l'été, l'automne ou le printemps.**

1.  Octobre _____
2.  Août _____
3.  Décembre _____
4.  Mai _____

# 13.3 Frequency

Here are some other words that come in handy when talking about time and the frequency of events:

| English | French | Pronunciation |
|---|---|---|
| Sometimes | **parfois** | *[paʁ-fwa]* |
| Often | **souvent** | *[soo-va~]* |
| Every day / each day | **chaque jour** | *[shak/joor]* |
| Every night / each night | **chaque nuit** | *[shak/n-wee]* |
| Every week / each week | **chaque semaine** | *[shak/sə-mayn]* |
| Every/ each… | **chaque** | *[shak]* |
| Once a day | **une fois par jour** | *[ahn/fwa/pahr/joor]* |
| Twice a day | **deux fois par jour** | *[dø/fwa/pahr/joor]* |
| Once a week | **une fois par semaine** | *[ahn/fwa/pahr/sə-mayn]* |
| Twice a week | **deux fois par semaine** | *[dø/fwa/pahr/sə-mayn]* |

| English | French | Pronunciation |
|---|---|---|
| Once a month | **une fois par mois** | [ahn/fwa/pahr/mwah] |
| Twice a month | **deux fois par mois** | [dø/fwa/pahr/mwah] |
| Once a year | **une fois par an** | [ahn/fwa/pahr/oh~] |
| Twice a year | **deux fois par an** | [dø/fwa/pahr/oh~] |

Here's how we can use these words:

| | | |
|---|---|---|
| **Sometimes I eat fish.** | → | Parfois je mange du poisson. |
| **She goes to the museum often.** | → | Elle va souvent au musée. |
| **Each evening, I drink a glass of wine.** | → | Chaque soir, je bois un verre de vin. |
| **We go to Paris once a year.** | → | Nous allons à Paris une fois par an. |

Now that you've mastered the art of time, dates, and seasons in French, let's put your knowledge to the test! Are you ready for the challenge?

## Practice 13.3

**A. Write the following sentences in French.**

1. Sometimes I eat a bowl of strawberries.

   _____

2. They go to the park often (co-ed.).

   _____

3. Is it winter? I want a cup of hot chocolate!

   _____

4. She arrives in August. In summer, we play chess every day.

   _____

5. It's evening! The party is at 7 PM.

   _____

6. Every morning, we eat a big breakfast together.

   _____

Speak Abroad
Academy

**B. Translate the following French sentences into English using everything you've learned so far.**

1. Chaque dimanche, il va à la boulangerie et mange un croissant.

   _____

2. Chaque été, nous allons à la plage. Il fait chaud en août !

   _____

3. On est en avril. Au printemps, j'aime lire dans le jardin.

   _____

4. En hiver, tu portes un élégant manteau noir. Tu es magnifique !

   _____

5. Il est midi et j'ai soif. Chaque après-midi, je bois un grand verre d'eau.

   _____

6. Chaque soir, elles regardent la télévision ensemble dans le salon.

   _____

**CHAPTER 14:**

# MORE ESSENTIALS
*YOU AND I, HER OR HIM*

## 14.1. Present Tense of *Parler*

As you continue to enhance your French communication skills, let me introduce you to the versatile verb *parler*. Unsurprisingly, it translates to both 'to speak' and 'to talk'. Get ready to weave this essential thread into the fabric of your growing language proficiency!

| Parler *to speak / to talk* | | | |
|---|---|---|---|
| je | **parle** | nous | **parlons** |
| tu | **parles** | vous | **parlez** |
| il | **parle** | ils | **parlent** |
| elle | | elles | |

Here's how we use it in a sentence…

| | | |
|---|---|---|
| **Yes, I speak French.** | → | Oui, je parle français. |
| **Each morning, she talks to the cow.** | → | Chaque matin, elle parle à la vache. |
| **He speaks French very well.** | → | Il parle très bien français. |
| **We talk to the flowers.** | → | Nous parlons aux fleurs. |
| **They are talking about photography** *(co-ed.).* | → | Ils parlent de photographie. |
| **They are talking about art** *(f.).* | → | Elles parlent d'art. |
| **You talk like a pirate** *(inf.).* | → | Tu parles comme un pirate. |
| **You speak French like a native** *(form.).* | → | Vous parlez français comme un natif. |

## Practice 14.1 *Parler*

**A. Let's practice the different conjugations of parler with the words for different languages.**

1. _____ français. (*I speak French.*)
2. _____ italien. (*You speak Italian – inf.*)
3. _____ espagnol. (*You speak Spanish – form.*)
4. _____ chinois. (*We speak Chinese.*)
5. _____ japonais. (*She speaks Japanese.*)
6. _____ anglais. (*He speaks English.*)
7. _____ allemand. (*They speak German – co-ed.m.*)
8. _____ portugais. (*They speak Portuguese – f.*)

**B. Write the following sentences in French using everything you've learned so far.**

1. We talk together every week.

   _____

2. They talk once a month (*co-ed.*).

   _____

3. Sometimes they speak Spanish (*f.*).

   _____

4. The intelligent man speaks French very well.

   _____

5. Each morning, you talk to the baby (inf.).

   _____

6. I don't speak Spanish.

   _____

7. She talks a lot.

   _____

8. Why do you talk to the cow?

   _____

**C. Translate the following sentences into English.**

1. J'aime parler à ma grand-mère. Elle est très drôle et intéressante.

   _____

2. Je parle à Jane toutes les semaines parce que nous sommes de bonnes amies.

   _____

3. Pourquoi parles-tu au chat ? Le chat ne parle pas anglais !

   _____

4. Qui parle ? Est-ce Emma et Esther ? Elles parlent trop.

   _____

5. Il parle aux chiens parce qu'il aime les animaux.

   _____

# 14.2 Conjunctions & Prepositions

Don't be intimidated by that big word! Conjunctions are some of the most common parts of everyday language. They connect other words, phrases, and clauses. For example, in that last sentence, 'and' was the conjunction, because it unites the rest of the sentence.

Some other examples of conjunctions are 'or' and 'but'. They allow us to say things like 'She came by, but she didn't come in'.

We've used some of these already, but it's time to learn even more! Consider the table below and then attempt the practice exercise:

| English | French | Pronunciation |
|---|---|---|
| And | **et** | [ay] |
| Or | **ou** | [oo] |
| But | **mais** | [may] |
| If | **si** | [see] |
| So | **alors** | [ah-lohr] |
| As / since / like a | **comme** | [kohm] |
| then | **puis** | [pwee] |

More essentials

Speak Abroad
Academy

## Practice 14.2 Conjunctions

**A. Let's start off simple. Fill in the blanks with the correct conjunction, either et, ou, or mais.**

1. Le garçon aime les fruits. Il mange une banane
   _____ une pomme.
2. Est-ce que Martin est médecin _____ avocat ?
3. Je veux cette robe, _____ elle est chère.
4. Est-ce que vous arrivez à huit heures _____ neuf heures ?
5. Il veut la voiture rouge, _____ sa femme aime la voiture rose.
6. Nous avons deux enfants : une fille _____ un fils.

**B. Circle or underline the correct conjunction in the following sentences.**

1. Il va à l'église, [ mais / puis / ou ] il va au bar.
2. La voiture est rouge [ et / alors / comme ] une tomate.
3. Elle est triste [ comme / alors / ou ] elle mange beaucoup de glace.
4. Je voudrais une grande bouteille de vin [ si / et / mais ] nous allons au restaurant.
5. Le garçon est grand [ comme / ou / puis ] son père.

# 14.3 More Prepositions

Let's learn the French words for some very useful time prepositions. These go hand-in-hand with what you've learned about dates and expressing the time.

| English | French | Pronunciation |
|---|---|---|
| During / while | **pendant** | [poh~-dah~] |
| After | **après** | [ah/pray] |
| Before | **avant** | [ah-vah~] |
| Except | **sauf** | [sohf] |
| Until | **jusqu'à** | [juhs/kah] |
| With | **avec** | [avayk] |
| Without | **sans** | [sah~] |
| For | **pour** | [poor] |

## Practice 14.3 Prepositions

### A. Choose the most appropriate preposition for the following sentences.

1.  [ Sauf / Après / Sans ] le dîner, nous regardons la télévision ensemble.
2.  Elle fait du sport [ avec / sans / jusqu'à ] ce soir.
3.  Je vais au musée [ sans / jusqu'à / pendant ] Jacques.
4.  Il aime la nourriture [ avant / après / sauf ] le fromage.
5.  Nous buvons une tasse de café [ avec / sauf / avant ] d'aller au parc.
6.  Ils parlent [ sans / sauf / pendant ] qu'ils font le jardinage.

### B. Translate the following sentences into English.

1.  Je vais à l'école tous les jours sauf le dimanche.

_____

2.  Il joue au football jusqu'à midi.

_____

3.  Vous mangez et buvez pendant un concert important.

_____

4.  Ils vont au musée avec une vieille femme.

_____

5.  Nous n'aimons pas manger avant de faire du sport.

_____

### C. Convert the following sentences in French.

1.  We eat dessert after dinner.

_____

2.  I'm making a cake without sugar.

_____

3.  They are talking during the movie (co-ed.).

_____

4.  She likes to read before breakfast.

_____

5.  He's drinking wine with an interesting man.

_____

**D. Use everything you've learned so far to identify which of the following sentences are grammatically incorrect.**

1. Ils mangent le dîner sauf le déjeuner.
2. Je sors pendant ma sœur.
3. Nous aimons tous les films sauf le dernier.
4. Vous allez à l'école pendant que je joue à la maison.
5. Il va à l'école sauf moi.
6. Tu sors avec tes amis.
7. Elle mange mais moi.
8. Vous sortez mais nous restons ici.

**E. Correct the grammatically incorrect sentences from the previous exercise by inserting the more appropriate word or fixing the sentence structure.**

1. _____
2. _____
3. _____
4. _____

## CHAPTER 15:

# POSSESSIVES & REFLEXIVES

*YOU AND I, HER OR HIM*

## 15.1 Possessive Adjectives

As you know, an adjective describes a noun. When the adjective is possessive, it describes who the noun belongs to and how. It's the difference between saying 'the cat' and *my* cat' or *'your* cat'. Take a look at the table below for the French words for these possessive adjectives. For now, we'll focus on describing singular nouns.

| | | |
|---|---|---|
| My | **mon** (m.) | **ma** (f.) |
| Your | **ton** | **ta** |
| His / her / its | **son** | **sa** |
| Our | **notre** | |
| Your (form.) | **votre** | |
| Their | **leur** | |

This is how we would use them in a sentence…

| | | |
|---|---|---|
| **This is my mother.** | → | C'est ma mère. |
| **She is your sister.** | → | Elle est ta soeur. |
| **He talks to his cat.** | → | Il parle à son chat. |
| **Our car is old.** | → | Notre voiture est vieille. |
| **Alice and Amy, is this your father?** | → | Alice et Amy, est-ce que c'est votre père ? |
| **Their new house is beautiful.** | → | Leur nouvelle maison est jolie. |

Watch out for this tricky part of French grammar! In front of feminine singular nouns beginning with a vowel (and most words beginning with 'h'), *ma* changes to *mon*, *ta* to *ton*, and *sa* to *son*. Why? It just makes them easier to say in French.

| | | |
|---|---|---|
| **my friend (m.)** | → | mon ami |
| **my friend (f.)** | → | mon amie |

## Practice 15.1.A

**Practice using possessive adjectives by converting the following into French.**

1. Her book _____
2. My dog _____
3. Our black car _____
4. Your *(inf.)* office _____
5. His glass of wine _____
6. Their beautiful cow _____
7. Your *(pl.)* intelligent daughter _____

## Practice 15.1.B

**Let's make these sentences a little more complex.**

1. Their father is my doctor. _____
2. Her jacket is red and my jacket is white. _____
3. He doesn't talk to his mother. _____
4. Their house is bigger than our house. _____
5. Your *(pl.)* son plays football with our son. _____
6. My sister likes to eat at your restaurant. _____

## Plural Possessive Adjectives

Whenever you're referring to multiple nouns, it's essential to use plural possessive adjectives. Thankfully, these are a little easier to use than singular possessive adjectives since the same word is used for both feminine and masculine nouns. Please consider the table below:

| | |
|---|---|
| My | **mes** |
| Your | **tes** |
| His / her / its | **ses** |
| Our | **nos** |
| Your (pl. + form.) | **vos** |
| Their | **leurs** |

This is how we would use them in a sentence...

**These are my dogs.** → Ce sont mes chiens.

**Her sisters are very kind.** → Ses sœurs sont très gentilles.

**His cars are expensive.** → Ses voitures sont chères.

**Our daughters are young.** → Nos filles sont jeunes.

**Their apples aren't ripe.** → Leurs pommes ne sont pas mûres.

---

**Tip:** Possessive adjectives must match the noun being possessed in gender and number, not the possessor. What happens if you're referring to your books? You say **mes livres**, even if there's only one of you. And if the person with the books is your friend? It's **ses livres**, even if there's one person holding the books.

---

You get the idea! Now we must test you!

## Practice 15.1.C

Convert the following from singular possessive to plural possessive.

**Example:** Mon chien. <u>Mes chiens.</u>

1. Ta tomate. _____
2. Ma fleur. _____
3. Son manteau. _____
4. Sa bière. _____
5. Leur voiture. _____
6. Notre fromage. _____
7. Votre canapé. _____

## Practice 15.1.D

Using everything you've learned about possessive adjectives, translate the following into French.

1. My sister doesn't like your sister.

   _____

2. Her cow is eating my flowers.

   _____

3. Where are your brothers?

_____

4. Your cats are in my garden.

_____

5. The intelligent woman is their lawyer.

_____

6. Our cars are too big for your garages.

_____

7. Sometimes our daughters go to the park together.

_____

## 15.2 Reflexive Pronouns & Verbs

When you use reflexive verbs, you're indicating that the subject performs an action to themselves. We call it 'reflexive' because it reflects back to the person performing the action. It's the difference between washing a plate and washing *yourself*.

In English, reflexive traits are indicated with words like *myself, yourself, herself, himself, itself, oneself, ourselves, themselves*.

In French, they are indicated by joining a reflexive pronoun to a verb. Reflexive pronouns are words like the following:

| | |
|---|---|
| Myself | **me** |
| Yourself | **te** |
| Himself / herself / itself | **se** |
| Ourselves | **nous** |
| Yourselves | **vous** |
| Themselves | **se** |

Don't forget to write **m'**, **t'** or **s'** if the following word starts with a vowel or **h**.

Here's how they work in French sentences.

| | | |
|---|---|---|
| **I wash myself.** | → | Je me lave. |
| **She washes herself.** | → | Elle se lave. |
| **He washes himself.** | → | Il se lave. |
| **We wash ourselves.** | → | Nous nous lavons. |
| **You wash yourself.** | → | Tu te laves. |
| **You wash yourselves.** | → | Vous vous lavez. |

**They wash themselves** (co-ed./m.).  →  Ils se lavent.

**They wash themselves** (f.).    →  Elles se lavent.

Yes, you're right! *Nous nous lavons* and *Vous vous lavez* sound a bit strange because of the repetition, but this is the right way to use reflexive French pronouns. Quirky, but accurate.

## Practice 15.2.A

**Fill in the blanks with the correct subject pronoun and reflexive pronoun.**

1. _____ habille. *(I get dressed – 'I dress myself'.)*
2. _____ lève. *(She wakes up – 'She wakes herself'.)*
3. _____ rase. *(He shaves himself.)*
4. _____ douchons. *(We shower ourselves.)*
5. _____ préparent. *(They get ready – 'They ready themselves' – f.)*
6. _____ regardes. *(You look at yourself – inf.)*
7. _____ calmez. *(You calm yourselves.)*
8. _____ cachent. *(They hide themselves – co-ed.)*

## Reflexive Verbs

Here are some basic reflexive verbs that will come in handy! Remember to replace **se** with the appropriate reflexive pronoun when you're using them in a sentence!

| English | French | Pronunciation |
|---|---|---|
| To wake oneself | **se réveiller** | [sə ray-vay-ay] |
| To get up | **se lever** | [sə lə-vay] |
| To brush one's teeth | **se brosser les dents** | [sə broh-say lay doh~] |
| To wash oneself | **se laver** | [sə lah-vay] |
| To shower oneself | **se doucher** | [sə doo-shay] |
| To shave oneself | **se raser** | [sə rah-zay] |
| To dress oneself | **s'habiller** | [sah-bee-yay] |
| To undress oneself | **se déshabiller** | [sə day-zah-bee-yay] |
| To prepare oneself | **se préparer** | [sə pray-pah-ray] |

Speak Abroad
Academy

| English | French | Pronunciation |
|---|---|---|
| To look at oneself | **se regarder** | *[sə rə-gahr-day]* |
| To ready oneself | **se préparer** | *[sə pray-pah-ray]* |
| To calm oneself | **se calmer** | *[sə kahl-may]* |
| To hide oneself | **se cacher** | *[sə kah-shay]* |
| To rest | **se reposer** | *[sə rə-poh-zay]* |

## Practice 15.2.B

**Read the following passage and answer the questions.**

*Une journée typique* (A typical day)

Chaque matin, Paul se réveille à huit heures. Il se lève à huit heures et quart et se brosse les dents, puis il se douche. Il se rase et s'habille. Après le petit-déjeuner, il va au bureau.

1. What time does Paul wake up? _____
2. How long after waking up does Paul get up?_____
3. What's the first thing Paul does after getting up? _____
4. What does Paul do right after he showers? _____
5. What does he do after he shaves? _____

## Practice 15.2.C

**Using the new reflexive verbs you just learned, convert the following into French.**

1. He undresses himself. _____
2. I prepare myself. _____
3. They (f.) look at themselves. _____
4. They (co-ed.) shave themselves. _____
5. You (inf.) calm yourself. _____
6. We wake up. _____
7. She dresses herself. _____
8. You (form./pl.) rest yourselves. _____

**Speak Abroad**
Academy

# 15.3 Present Tense of *Pouvoir*

To fully prepare you for your French journey, here's one more important French verb. *Pouvoir* means 'to be able to' or in other words, 'can'. It's an apt verb to learn in this final section, since you are becoming *able to* speak French!

| Pouvoir *to be able to / can* | | | |
|---|---|---|---|
| je | **peux** | nous | **pouvons** |
| tu | **peux** | vous | **pouvez** |
| il | **peut** | ils | **peuvent** |
| elle | | elles | |

We generally put *pouvoir* in front of other verbs to express that one *can* do something. For example...

| | | |
|---|---|---|
| **I can go to the party tonight.** | → | Je peux aller à la fête ce soir. |
| **She can drink a lot.** | → | Elle peut boire beaucoup. |
| **You can come with me** *(form./pl.)*. | → | Vous pouvez venir avec moi. |
| **We can bake a delicious cake.** | → | Nous pouvons faire un délicieux gâteau. |
| **They can be our friends** *(f.)*. | → | Elles peuvent être nos amies. |
| **He can play football like a professional.** | → | Il peut jouer au football comme un professionnel. |
| **You can wake up in the afternoon** *(inf.)*. | → | Tu peux te réveiller dans l'après-midi. |
| **They can eat a lot of cheese** *(co-ed, m.)*. | → | Ils peuvent manger beaucoup de fromage. |

## Practice 15.3

**A. Let's practice different conjugations of pouvoir.**

1. _____ manger ta tomate. (*You can* eat your tomato – inf.)

2. _____ y aller quand je veux. (*I can* go whenever I want.)

3. _____ dîner avec nous. (*They can* have dinner with us – f.)

4. _____ avoir nos vieilles chaussures. (*They can* have our old shoes – co-ed.)

5. _____ boire toute la bouteille de vin. (*You can* drink the whole bottle of wine – form./pl.)

Possessives & reflexives

6. _____ porter des chapeaux roses à la fête. (*We can* wear pink hats to the party.)

7. _____ avoir la vache. (*She can* have the cow.)

8. _____ jouer aux jeux vidéo chez nous. (*He can* play video games at our house.)

## B. Now, let's practice saying 'cannot' with pouvoir. Convert the following affirmative sentences into negative sentences.

**Example:** Je peux marcher. <u>Je ne peux pas marcher.</u>

1. Je peux aller au musée. _____

2. Tu peux manger du fromage. _____

3. Elle peut prendre (*to take*) le croissant. _____

4. Il peut parler à la vache. _____

5. Vous pouvez préparer le petit-déjeuner. _____

6. Nous pouvons manger dans le jardin. _____

7. Ils peuvent parler français. _____

8. Ils peuvent porter des chaussettes à la plage. _____

## C. Let's practice everything you've learned so far. Write the following sentences in French.

1. It's Sunday today. There are two men in front of my house. They are my friends. We are going to the museum together.

   _____

2. At 5 PM, I get ready for the party. I'm wearing a beautiful black dress and white shoes.

   _____

3. For dessert tonight, we have cake. Do you want ice cream on top of the cake?

   _____

4. They are a kind family. They have three intelligent daughters and a beautiful house, but I don't like their dog.

   _____

5. My brother likes poetry and my sister likes tennis. And me? I like our cat.

   _____

6. In the spring, they (m.) go to the park. In the summer, they (m.) go to the beach. It's too hot, so I go to church.

   _____

# CONCLUSION

As we close this book, we hope that your journey through the foundational aspects has been an enriching and enjoyable experience for you as it has been for us to guide you on. Our aim was to ultimately help you master a language that you can feel completely at ease with while communicating. A language that can help you with building new connections and foster a deeper sense of the self.

From the basic building blocks of pronouns and greetings to the complexities of negations and possessives, each chapter was designed to bring you closer to fluency, one step at a time. May the knowledge you've gained serve as a sturdy bridge to your future endeavours in French, whether they be in conversation, travel, or further studies.

Remember, the path to mastery is a continuous journey, and every word you learn is a step forward. *Bon voyage* on your linguistic adventure!

**LEARN FRENCH
GRAMMAR WORKBOOK**

Speak Abroad
Academy

# ANSWER KEY

## CHAPTER 1
### 1.1 Pronouns

| A | 1. Nous | 2. Je | 3. Elles | 4. Ils | 5. Tu | 6. Vous | 7. Nous | 8. Ils |
|---|---|---|---|---|---|---|---|---|
| B | 1. Je | 2. Nous | 3. Vous | 4. Vous | 5. Ils | 6. Tu | | |
| C | 1. Ils | 2. Vous | 3. Vous | 4. Nous | 5. Il | 6. Elle | | |
| D | 1. Tu | 2. Tu | 3. Vous | 4. Vous | 5. Tu | | | |
| | 6. Vous | 7. Vous | 8. Tu | 9. Tu | 10. Vous | | | |
| E | 1. Tu | 2. Vous | 3. Vous | 4. Vous | 5. Vous | | | |

### 1.3 Language Etiquette

| A | 1. C | 2. D | 3. B | 4. E | 5. F | 6. A |
|---|---|---|---|---|---|---|
| B | 1. Salut/Bonjour | 2. Bonjour | 3. Salut/Bonjour | 4. Bonsoir | 5. Bonjour | |
| C | 1. A | 2. C | 3. D | 4. B | 5. E | |
| D | 1. E | 2. C | 3. D | 4. A | 5. B | |
| E | 1. ça va ? | 2. et toi ? | 3. bien | 4. À | 5. Au revoir | |

## CHAPTER 2
### 2.1 Gender of Nouns

| 1. La | 2. L' | 3. La | 4. Le | 5. Le | 6. Le |
|---|---|---|---|---|---|
| 7. La | 8. L' | 9. La | 10. L' | 11. La | 12. Le |

### 2.2 Plural Nouns

| A | 1. Les hommes | 2. Les amies | 3. Les conversations | 4. Les animaux | 5. Les systèmes |
|---|---|---|---|---|---|
| | 6. Les petits | 7. Les maisons | 8. Les trains | 9. Les villes | 10. Les médecins |
| B | 1. La vérité | 2. La télévision | 3. La main | 4. La chienne | 5. Le crayon |
| | 6. La fille | 7. La radio | 8. La salade | | |

### 2.3 Indefinite Article

| A | 1. Des grands-pères | 2. Des conversations | 3. Des chiens | 4. Des femmes | 5. Des étudiants |
|---|---|---|---|---|---|
| | 6. Des médecins | 7. Des hôtels | 8. Des trains | 9. Des crayons | 10. Des villes |
| B | 1. Les étudiants | 2. Les planètes | 3. Un médecin | 4. Des photos | 5. La langue |
| | 6. Les touristes | 7. Des amis | 8. Une tomate | 9. Une conversation | 10. Des vérités |

| C | 1. La | 2. des | 3. la | 4. une | 5. des | 6. le | 7. un | 8. les |
|---|---|---|---|---|---|---|---|---|

| D | 1. The book | 2. The house | 3. The flowers | 4. The young boy | 5. The brothers | 6. The coffee |
|---|---|---|---|---|---|---|
| | 7. The train | 8. The planets | 9. A cat | 10. Some dogs | 11. The phone | 12. The hands |
| | 13. A program | 14. Some systems | 15. The books | 16. The city | | |

| E | 1. La | 2. des | 3. une | 4. Le | 5. une | 6. les | 7. le | 8. un | 9. les |
|---|---|---|---|---|---|---|---|---|---|
| F | 1. une | 2. une | 3. la | 4. La | 5. Le | 6. d'une | 7. les | 8. un | |

## CHAPTER 3
### 3.1 Singular Adjectives

| A | 1. grande | 2. pauvre | 3. loyal | 4. bel | 5. difficile | 6. bon | 7. heureux | 8. intéressant | 9. forte | 10. faible |
|---|---|
| B | 1. petite | 2. excellente | 3. petite | 4. gentil | 5. vieux | 6. mauvais | 7. intelligente | 8. loyale | 9. travailleur | 10. grosse |
| C | 1. Difficile | 2. Grand | 3. Bon | 4. Sympathique | 5. Grand | 6. Faible |

### 3.2 Plural Adjectives

| | |
|---|---|
| A | 1. Les grandes tomates \| 2. Les petits hommes \| 3. Les chiens intelligents \| 4. Les filles fortes \| 5. Les personnes travailleuses \| 6. Les petites villes \| 7. Les chats minces \| 8. Les femmes heureuses \| 9. Les livres difficiles \| 10. Les excellentes nourritures |
| B | 1. excellents \| 2. travailleuse \| 3. belle \| 4. petits \| 5. jolis \| 6. bonnes \| 7. gros \| 8. sympathiques |

### 3.3 Nationality

| 1. américaine | 2. française | 3. anglaise | 4. italienne | 5. espagnol | 6. allemande |
|---|---|---|---|---|---|

### 3.4 Describing a Person

| | |
|---|---|
| A | 1. jeune \| 2. petit \| 3. intéressant \| 4. drôle \| 5. intelligent \| 6. loyal |
| B | 1. intelligente \| 2. grand \| 3. français \| 4. gros \| 5. belle \| 6. gentille \| 7. anglais \| 8. vieux |
| C | 1. Marc est français \| 2. Anna est anglaise \| 3. Le garçon est grand \| 4. La fille est intelligente \| 5. L'homme est gentil \| 6. La femme est belle |
| D | 1. français \| 2. américaine \| 3. anglais \| 4. italien \| 5. française \| 6. anglaise |

## CHAPTER 4
### 4.1 Adjectives

| | |
|---|---|
| A | 1. nouvelle \| 2. joyeuse \| 3. bon \| 4. gros \| 5. petit \| 6. méchant \| 7. vieux \| 8. chère \| 9. grand \| 10. lente \| 11. bruyant \| 12. long |
| B | 1. jaune \| 2. bleue \| 3. orange \| 4. blanche \| 5. noire \| 6. gris \| 7. vert \| 8. rose \| 9. marron \| 10. rouge |
| C | 1. lent – rapide \| 2. noir – blanche \| 3. grande – petit \| 4. gros – mince \| 5. vieux – jeune \| 6. riche – pauvre |
| D | 1. grand et vieux \| 2. laide et pauvre \| 3. vieille et petite \| 4. joyeux et rapide \| 5. facile |

### 4.2 Demonstrative Adjectives

| | | | | | | | |
|---|---|---|---|---|---|---|---|
| A | 1. Ce manteau est beau \| 2. Ces chaussures sont chères \| 3. Cette chemise est douce \| 4. Ces bottes sont élégantes \| 5. Ce chapeau est propre | | | | | | |
| B | 1. ce – Ce | 2. Cette | 3. Cette | 4. Ce | 5. Cette | 6. Ces | 7. Cet | 8. Ces |

### 4.3 Describing Nouns

| | | | | | |
|---|---|---|---|---|---|
| A | 1. Cette | 2. Ce – cet | 3. Cette – ces | 4. Cette | |
| B | 1. sont | 2. est – sont | 3. est | 4. sont – est | 5. est |
| | 6. sont – sont | 7. sont | 8. est | 9. sont | 10. sont – est |

## CHAPTER 5

| | |
|---|---|
| A | 1. Thomas et Adeline \| 2. Thomas et Adeline \| 3. Paul \| 4. Parce qu'ils sont des touristes et New York est une grande ville \| 5. Une carte |
| B | 1. est italien \| 2. est mexicaine \| 3. est américain \| 4. est allemand \| 5. est française \| 6. est espagnol \| 7. est portugais \| 8. est anglais \| 9. est autrichien\| |
| C | 1. sommes \| 2. es \| 3. sont \| 4. suis – es \| 5. est \| 6. sont \| 7. sont \| 8. sommes \| 9. est \| 10. est \| 11. êtes \| 12. êtes \| 13. suis \| 14. est \| 15. est – est \| 16. sont \| 17. êtes \| 18. sont \| 19. es \| 20. suis |
| D | 1. Nous sommes \| 2. Ils sont \| 3. Je suis \| 4. Tu es \| 5. Vous êtes \| 6. Nous sommes \| 7. Elles sont \| 8. Ils sont \| 9. Je suis \| 10. Ils sont \| 11. Tu es \| 12. Vous êtes |
| E | 1. Anna est au musée. \| 2. Nous sommes dehors. \| 3. Elsa et Jane sont à l'école. \| 4. Ils sont à la banque. \| 5. Il est au supermarché. \| 6. Elle est très bruyante. \| 7. Nous sommes dans la voiture. \| 8. Tu es heureux. \| 9. Je suis jeune et beau. \| 10. Vous êtes très intelligent. \| 11. Georges est vieux. \| 12. Vous êtes au supermarché. |
| F | 1. est \| 2. sommes – la voiture \| 3. est – est – la maison \| 4. suis – est \| 5. est – Elle est française \| 6. es – suis |
| G | 1. Anglais \| 2. Américain \| 3. Anglaise \| 4. Anglais \| 5. Espagnole \| 6. Français \| 7. Japonaise \| 8. Japonais |
| H | 1. Chauffeur \| 2. Peintre \| 3. Cheffe cuisinière \| 4. Écrivain \| 5. Médecin \| 6. Écrivain \| 7. Écrivaine \| 8. Médecin |

Speak Abroad
Academy

| I | 1. The dress is beautiful and very expensive. |
|---|---|
| | 2. The man in the car is a doctor. |
| | 3. The teachers are very intelligent. And the students? They are intelligent too! |
| | 4. This house is big and that house is small. |
| | 5. These dogs are old, but they're fast. |
| | 6. The men are at a party and the women are at the restaurant. |
| | 7. Today, the girl is tired. She's very hard-working. |
| | 8. The French woman is a lawyer. The American man is a driver. They are friends. |
| | 9. This shirt is black and beautiful. That shirt is white and ugly, but it's cheap! |
| | 10. The cat is in the garden. Oh no! The cow is in the garden too. |
| | 11. He is very quiet. He's a pharmacist and the pharmacy is quiet. |

## CHAPTER 6
### 6.1 Present Tense Avoir

| A | 1. Nous avons | 2. J'ai | 3. Tu as | 4. J'ai | 5. Elle a | |
|---|---|---|---|---|---|---|
| | 6. Ils ont | 7. Il a | 8. Elles ont | 9. Vous avez | 10. Nous avons | |
| B | 1. je suis | 2. Vous avez | 3. Il a – Il est | 4. Elle a – elle est | 5. Je suis | 6. Ils ont |
| | 7. Nous sommes | 8. J'ai | 9. Tu es – tu as | 10. Elles sont – elles sont | 11. Nous avons | |
| C | 1. J'ai | 2. Ils ont – ils ont | 3. Elle a – il a | 4. Vous avez | 5. Elles ont | |
| | 6. Nous avons | 7. J'ai | 8. Tu as | | | |
| D | 1. Trois | 2. Quatre | 3. Zéro | 4. Paul | 5. Paul. Cinq | 6. Francine |

### 6.2 Age

| A | 1. J'ai vingt-cinq ans. \| 2. J'ai trente ans. \| 3. J'ai trente-sept ans. \| 4. J'ai quarante ans. \| 5. J'ai quarante-et-un ans. \| 6. J'ai quatre-vingt-dix ans. |
|---|---|
| B | 1. Elle a vingt ans. \| 2. Nous avons quinze ans. \| 3. Ils ont quatre-vingt-cinq ans. \| 4. Elles ont quatre-vingt-six ans. \| 5. Tu as vingt-neuf ans. \| 6. Vous avez soixante ans. \| 7. J'ai trente-huit ans. \| 8. Il a cent ans. |
| C | 1. Elle est jeune. \| 2. Il est vieux. \| 3. Nous sommes jeunes. \| 4. Nous sommes vieux/vieilles. \| 5. Ils sont vieux. \| 6. Je suis jeune. \| 7. Tu es jeune. \| 8. Elles sont vieilles. \| 9. Elle est jeune. \| 10. Il est vieux. |

### 6.3 Quantity

| A | B | C |
|---|---|---|
| 1. Marie has ten cats. She has too many cats! | 1. a moins de chats que Bob. | 1. Six |
| 2. I have more children than Jennifer. | 2. a plus de filles que Charlie. | 2. Neuf |
| 3. He has a lot of uncles and aunts. They are too noisy. | 3. a moins d'argent que Daniel. | 3. Isabelle |
| 4. They have a little money. | 4. a plus de livres qu'Emily. | 4. Isabelle |
| 5. We have too many problems. | 5. J'ai moins de chiens que Freddie. | 5. Deux cents |
| 6. Nina has less friends than Natasha. | 6. J'ai plus de voitures que George. | 6. Deux mille |
| 7. James has ten dollars. Jim has fifteen dollars. Jim has more money than James. | | |
| 8. Daniel and Emily have thirty dollars. We have less money than Daniel and Emily. | | |

## CHAPTER 7
### 7.1 Demonstratives

| A | B |
|---|---|
| 1. Il y a une fleur dans le jardin. | 1. Il y a des femmes dans le jardin. |
| 2. Il y a un ordinateur sur la table. | 2. Il y a des clés sur la table. |
| 3. Il y a une femme devant la voiture. | 3. Il y a trois chats sous la voiture. |
| 4. Il y a un chat derrière la maison. | 4. Il y a un grand homme dehors. |
| 5. Il y a une fille sous la table. | 5. Il y a cinq grands hommes dehors. |
| | 6. Il y a des fleurs rouges et jaunes dans le jardin. |

### 7.2 Household Vocabulary

| | |
|---|---|
| A | 1. The walls are white. \| 2. The house is small, but the garden is big. \| 3. I like the kitchen. It's beautiful and new. \| 4. She's in the living room. \| 5. We are in the office. \| 6. The family is in the dining room. \| 7. The black car is in the garage. The red car is outside. \| 8. The woman is in the bathroom. |
| B | 1. The house is big. There are eight bedrooms and four bathrooms. \| 2. It's a beautiful day. There are flowers in the garden. \| 3. There's a cat inside the basket. \| 4. There are books on the floor. \| 5. There are red cars outside. \| 6. There's a black cat in front of the house. |
| C | 1. I have two cats and two dogs. The cats are on the bed. The dogs are in the garden. 2. I am a driver. I have three cars in the garage. One is black. Two are red. 3. Caroline is a friendly girl. She has thirty friends and they are friendly too. 4. There's a tall man in the garage. It's my father. And the friendly woman in the kitchen? That's my mother. 5. The woman in the restaurant is old. She's eighty-six years old and she has eight daughters. 6. These blue shoes are new. And these green shoes are new too. I have too many shoes. |

### 7.3 Aller

| | |
|---|---|
| A | 1. Je vais \| 2. Elle va \| 3. Il va \| 4. Nous allons \| 5. Tu vas \| 6. Vous allez \| 7. Vous allez \| 8. Ils vont \| 9. Elles vont |
| B | 1. Tu vas \| 2. Il va \| 3. Elles vont \| 4. Je vais \| 5. Vous allez \| 6. Elle va \| 7. Ils vont \| 8. Nous allons \| 9. Vous allez \| 10. Je vais |
| C | 1. It's a beautiful day. We are going to the park. \| 2. The supermarket is behind the bakery. \| 3. I'm in the garden and you're going to work. \| 4. The woman in the car is going to the bank. \| 5. Emily and Daniel are going to the museum with their friends. \| 6. My mother is at home. My father is going to the supermarket. \| 7. The family is going to the restaurant. \| 8. He's going to the bar in his new car. \| 9. There's a dog in front of the restaurant. \| 10. I'm going to the house! There's a cow outside. |

### 7.4 Correct Sentences

| A | 1. X | 2. ✓ | 3. X | 4. X | 5. ✓ | 6. X | 7. ✓ | 8. ✓ | 9. ✓ | 10. X |
|---|---|---|---|---|---|---|---|---|---|---|
| B | 1. Je vais bien. | | 2. C'est un beau chien/ Ce sont des beaux chiens. | | 3. Ces femmes me plaisent, elles sont belles. | | 4. Nous avons/ Vous avez un examen. | | 5. Il est médecin. | |
| C | 1. va | 2. est | 3. ont | 4. avez | 5. allons | 6. a | | | | |

## CHAPTER 8
### 8.1 Faire

| | |
|---|---|
| A | 1. Tu fais \| 2. Je fais \| 3. Nous faisons \| 4. Ils font \| 5. Il fait \| 6. Elles font \| 7. Elle fait \| 8. Vous faites |
| B | 1. We are making a cake in the kitchen. \| 2. The tall woman is exercising in the garden. \| 3. The two friends do photography in the park. \| 4. The kind man is doing the dishes. \| 5. Emily and Erica are at the shops. They are shopping. |

### 8.2 Weather

| A | 1. Il pleut | 2. Il fait froid | 3. Il fait chaud | 4. Il pleut | 5. Il fait chaud |
|---|---|---|---|---|---|
| B | 1. A | 2. A | 3. A | | |

### 8.3 Vouloir

| 1. Tu veux | 2. Je veux | 3. Elle veut | 4. Elles veulent | 5. Nous voulons | 6. Ils veulent |
|---|---|---|---|---|---|

### 8.4 Conditional Vouloir

| A | 1. Il voudrait des fleurs. | 2. Nous voudrions trois cafés, s'il vous plaît. | 3. Je voudrais une chemise bleue et une jupe blanche. | 4. Ils voudraient une table | 5. Elle voudrait un manteau noir. |
|---|---|
| B | 1. The grandmother. | 2. A new cat. | 3. Next to the bakery. |
| C | 1. We're shopping at the supermarket. Fruits are expensive! | 2. The weather is good. There are flowers in the park. I want to go to the park. | 3. He's making the bed. You're doing the dishes. And me? I'm at a bar with friends. | 4. It's raining. The new clothes are wet. | 5. It's cold today! I would like a hot coffee. She wants coffee too. |

### 8.5 Porter

| A | 1. Il porte | 2. Tu portes | 3. Elles portent | 4. Elle porte | 5. Je porte | 6. Nous portons | 7. Ils portent |
|---|---|
| B | 1. It's a beautiful day. I'm wearing a new shirt and we're going to an expensive restaurant. |
| | 2. I'm wearing a brown jacket, but I would like a black jacket. |
| | 3. It's hot today. I'm wearing sunglasses and shorts. I'm going to the park with friends. |
| | 4. She wears expensive clothes, but these clothes are old and ugly. |
| | 5. I would like four small yellow hats, please. They are for my cats! |

## CHAPTER 9
### 9.1 Food

| A | 1. A salad | 2. Bread and cheese | 3. A beer | 4. Fish and vegetables | 5. Coffee with sugar | 6. An apple | 7. Chicken and beef | 8. Tea with milk |
|---|---|
| B | 1. Ten eggs | 2. Five apples | 3. Fifteen potatoes | 4. Three bananas | 5. Thirty-five lemons | 6. Nineteen mushrooms | 7. Two beers | 8. Twenty peaches |
| C | 1. Je voudrais un café avec du lait et du sucre. | 2. Je voudrais une salade. | 3. Nous voudrions de la viande et des légumes. | 4. Il voudrait une bière et elle voudrait un jus. 5. Elle voudrait des champignons dans la salade. | 6. Ils voudraient du pain et du beurre |
| D | 1. She would like ice cream on top of the cake. | 2. He would like fish and vegetables for dinner. | 3. I would like a beer with dinner. | 4. We would like ice cream for dessert. | 5. I would like strawberries and chocolate. | 6. They would like eggs, ham, and bread. |

### 9.2 Units of Food

| A | 1. A spoonful of sugar | 2. A cup of milk | 3. Two cups of milk | 4. A handful of strawberries | 5. A plate of sausages | 6. A glass of wine | 7. A bottle of wine | 8. A bowl of cherries |
|---|---|
| B | 1. There's a cup of coffee on the table. | 2. There's a plate of eggs and ham in the kitchen. | 3. There's tea in the cup, but I would like a coffee. | 4. There are five bottles of beer on the table in the garden. | 5. There's a bottle of wine in the bedroom. It's for you and me. |

### 9.3 Manger

| A | 1. Elles mangent | 2. Tu manges | 3. Je mange | 4. Ils mangent | 5. Elle mange | 6. Il mange | 7. Vous mangez | 8. Nous mangeons |
|---|---|
| B | 1. Je mange une pomme au petit-déjeuner. | 2. Michael et Marie mangent ensemble. | 3. Nous mangeons une grande assiette de poisson. C'est délicieux ! | 4. Ils mangent dans le jardin ce soir. | 5. Tu manges dehors avec la vache ce soir. | 6. Elle mange une poignée de fraises. | 7. Il mange de la glace pour le dessert. |

### 9.4 Boire

| A | 1. Every night, he drinks too much beer and I eat too much cake. |
|---|---|
| | 2. We are at the restaurant. There's a big plate of beef on the table. It's delicious! |
| | 3. For breakfast, I drink coffee with sugar and milk. Louis drinks a glass of apple juice. |
| | 4. There's a plate of eggs and sausages in the kitchen. It's for you! |
| | 5. Andy and Angela drink a lot of wine. Bob and I, we eat a lot of salad. |
| B | 1. Un restaurant français populaire | 2. Huit | 3. Ils travaillent ensemble | 4. Quatre bouteilles de vin | 5. De la viande de bœuf, du poulet, du poisson et des légumes |

## CHAPTER 10
### 10.1 Aimer

| 1. aimes | 2. aime | 3. aimons | 4. aimez | 5. aime | 6. aime | 7. aiment | 8. aiment |
|---|---|---|---|---|---|---|---|

### 10.2 Hobbies

| 1. Julia aime la poésie. | 2. Nous aimons beaucoup la musique. | 3. J'aime les romans de fiction. |
|---|---|---|
| 4. Ils aiment la photographie. | 5. Il aime les jeux de société. | 6. Tu aimes beaucoup l'art. |

### 10.3 Faire + Hobbies

| A | 1. Il aime jouer aux échecs. \| 2. Nous aimons danser dans la cuisine. \| 3. Elle aime pâtisser. \| 4. Ils aiment jouer aux jeux vidéo. \| 5. J'aime jouer aux jeux de société. \| 6. Tu aimes écouter de la musique et j'aime danser. |
|---|---|
| B | 1. They like to exercise together in the garden. \| 2. She likes to do sports at school. \| 3. We like to listen to music in the morning. \| 4. He likes to eat cake. I like to make cakes. \| 5. I like to watch television with my friend. \| 6. They like to go shopping in Paris. \| 7. You like to do gardening. \| 8. You like to read interesting books. |
| C | 1. He has a television because he likes movies. \| 2. Rachel likes meat. She would like a plate of chicken, please. \| 3. I like to play soccer with the white dog. \| 4. We like to play video games with beautiful women. \| 5. They like to play chess in the garden. \| 6. They like flowers. Every day, they like to garden together. |

### 10.4. Dislikes

| A | 1. Tu n'aimes pas les \| 2. Je n'aime pas le \| 3. Nous n'aimons pas les \| 4. Vous n'aimez pas \| 5. Il n'aime pas \| 6. Elle n'aime pas \| 7. Ils n'aiment pas \| 8. Elles n'aiment pas |
|---|---|
| B | 1. Je n'aime pas les musées. \| 2. Elle n'aime pas les chats noirs. \| 3. Nous n'aimons pas le vin. \| 4. Ils n'aiment pas manger dans des restaurants chers. \| 5. Vous n'aimez pas regarder la télévision. \| 6. Ils n'aiment pas manger de la glace. \| 7. Vous n'aimez pas jouer au tennis. \| 8. Il n'aime pas lire dans le jardin. |
| C | 1. Ils aiment cuisiner. \| 2. Il aime porter des chaussures. \| 3. J'aime danser. \| 4. Elle aime boire de la bière. \| 5. Vous aimez les vaches. \| 6. Ils aiment manger du fromage. \| 7. Nous aimons regarder la télévision le soir. \| 8. Tu aimes le nouveau chat. |
| D | 1. We don't like the black sofa in the living room. \| 2. There are three dogs in front of the house. I like the black dog. \| 3. They don't like to play soccer in the park. \| 4. The young man likes to cycle. He is very fast. \| 5. I am very happy. There are twenty books on the table. I like to read. \| 6. She likes to play basketball, but I don't like sports. I like to play chess. |
| E | 1. Il veut un grand jardin. Il aime jardiner. <br> 2. Elle mange beaucoup, mais elle n'aime pas les légumes. <br> 3. J'aime la couleur jaune. Je n'aime pas la couleur noire. <br> 4. Tu aimes la femme riche. J'aime l'homme loyal. <br> 5. Nous aimons le pain à la boulangerie. Nous n'aimons pas le pain au restaurant. <br> 6. Ils n'aiment pas regarder la télévision ensemble. |

## CHAPTER 11
### 11.1 Ne... pas

| A | 1. Je ne suis pas une vache. \| 2. Je ne mange pas de gâteau. \| 3. Je ne vais pas à la gare. \| 4. Je n'ai pas de gentil frère. \| 5. Je ne veux pas de nouveau chat. \| 6. Je ne voudrais pas de bol de cerises. 7. Je ne porte pas de chapeau bleu. \| 8. Je n'aime pas les fleurs. \| 9. Je ne bois pas de verre de vin. |
|---|---|
| B | 1. Vous n'aimez pas le parapluie jaune. \| 2. Il ne veut pas de verre d'eau. \| 3. Elle ne va pas sortir. \| 4. Elles ne portent pas de nouveaux vêtements. \| 5. Nous ne buvons pas beaucoup de jus d'orange. \| 6. Ils ne sont pas des hommes riches. \| 7. Elle n'est pas triste. \| 8. Nous n'avons pas deux fils. \| 9. Vous n'allez pas à l'école. |
| C | 1. Elle ne veut pas de la petite maison. \| 2. Je ne veux pas lire un livre. \| 3. Nous ne mangeons pas de viande. \| 4. Ils n'ont pas de chat blanc. \| 5. Je ne suis pas médecin. \| 6. Il ne mange pas de poisson. \| 7. Tu ne vas pas sortir. |

| D | 1. Je mange pas de viande.\| 4. Nous ne voulons sortir.\| 6. Ils sont pas grands. |
|---|---|
| E | 1. Je ne mange pas de viande. \| 2. Nous ne voulons pas sortir. \| 3. Ils ne sont pas grands. |

### 11.2. Ne... jamais

| A | 1. Elle n'a jamais d'argent. \| 2. Le grand homme ne va jamais au supermarché. \| 3. Je ne mange jamais de viande. \| 4. Nous n'allons jamais à l'école. \| 5. Ils ne prennent jamais le petit-déjeuner ensemble. \| 6. Vous ne buvez jamais de bière. \| 7. Elles ne font jamais le lit. \| 8. Tu ne vas jamais à l'église. |
|---|---|
| B | 1.<br>3.<br>5. |
| C | 1. Il ne travaille jamais. \| 2. Je ne sors jamais de l'école. \| 3. Vous n'aimez pas aller avec moi. |
| D | 1. Deux ans \| 2. Noisy (bruyant) \| 3. Les légumes \| 4. Au restaurant \| 5. Des vacances |
| E | 1. She doesn't like to eat dessert. She eats salads.<br>2. I have five children; I never go to the movies!<br>3. He likes to go to expensive restaurants, but he never has any money.<br>4. You like sad poetry. You are never happy!<br>5. We never drink beer. We would like to have two glasses of wine. |

## CHAPTER 12
### 12.1 *Est-ce que*

| A | 1. Est-ce qu'il a six chats ? \| 2. Est-ce que nous aimons la voiture orange ? \| 3. Est-ce qu'elle va à la gare ? \| 4. Est-ce qu'ils sont jeunes ? \| 5. Est-ce que nous avons une belle voiture ? \| 6. Est-ce que Jenny a plus d'argent que James ? |
|---|---|
| B | 1. Est-ce que tu aimes les chiens ? \| 2. Est-ce que c'est un vieil homme ? \| 3. Est-ce qu'ils vont au restaurant français ? \| 4. Est-ce que vous êtes riches ? \| 5. Est-ce que tu as une grande maison ? \| 6. Est-ce qu'ils vont aller à la boulangerie ? |

### 12.2 Inversions

| A | 1. As-tu une voiture ? \| 2. Boit-il du vin ? \| 3. Aimez-vous le nouveau restaurant ? \| 4. Fait-elle du sport ? \| 5. Aiment-elles jouer au football ? \| 6. Aimez-vous lire ? |
|---|---|
| B | 1. Faites-vous toujours du sport les week-ends ? \| 2. Dois-je finir mon examen ce matin ? \| 3. Est-elle contente de venir ici ? \| 4. Allons-nous tous au même restaurant ? \| 5. Va-t-il au bureau le samedi ? \| 6. Es-tu content de regarder ce film avec moi ? |

### 12.3. Who, What, Where

| 1. Mon école est en face de l'église. | 2. C'est mon père. | 3. Le violet est ma couleur préférée. |
|---|---|---|
| 4. Ma femme est une écrivaine. | 5. Il est à côté du nouveau restaurant. | |

### 12.4. When, How, Why

| 1. Il commence ce soir. | 2. Mon mari va très bien. | 3. Elle va venir ce soir. |
|---|---|---|
| 4. Quand nous allons au restaurant français. | | 5. Mon frère ne va pas bien. |

### 12.5. Pourquoi

| 1. I have a cat because I like cats. | 2. He's outside because he doesn't like the dog. | 3. She wants the black car because the white car is ugly. |
|---|---|---|
| 4. You are wearing shorts because it's hot and sunny. | 5. We play chess a lot because we're intelligent. | 6. You eat five bowls of ice cream because you're sad. |

### 12.6. Expressions + Prepositions

| A | 1. Who does Jacob go to the restaurant with? \| 2. She wants a jacket? Which one? \| 3. Who am I making a cake for? \| 4. Whose house are you in? \| 5. Where do they come from? \| 6. What are we cooking with? |
|---|---|
| B | 1. Sasha \| 2. À la boulangerie \| 3. Une chemise noire et un jean \| 4. Derrière l'église \| 5. De Max |

## CHAPTER 13
### 13.1 Asking for Time

| | |
|---|---|
| A | 1. Correct \| 2. X \| 3. Correct \| 4. X |
| B | 1. À quelle heure est le film ? \| 2. À quelle heure est le concert ? \| 3. À quelle heure est la fête d'anniversaire ? \| 4. À quelle heure est la classe des arts ? \| 5. À quelle heure est le pique-nique ? |
| C | 1. 1p.m. \| 2. 8:35 p.m. \| 3. 8:20 a.m. \| 4. 11:15 p.m. \| 5. 7:30 a.m. \| 6. 6:33p.m. |
| D | 1. Huit heures vingt \| 2. Dix heures quarante \| 3. Six heures dix \| 4. Quinze heures cinq \| 5. Dix-neuf heures cinquante  \| 6. Vingt-trois heures dix-huit |
| E | 1. Neuf heures \| 2. Dix heures et demie \| 3. Midi \| 4. Une heure et quart \| 4. Deux heures moins le quart \| 6. Quatre heures et demie \| 7. Huit heures moins le quart \| 8. Dix heures et quart |

### 13.2 Expressing Date

| A | 1. octobre | 2. février | 3. juin | 4. avril | 5. août | 6. juillet | 7. mercredi |
|---|---|---|---|---|---|---|---|
| | 8. vendredi | 9. mardi | 10. samedi | 11. hier | 12. demain | 13. aujourd'hui | 14. le mois prochain |

| B | 1. On est jeudi aujourd'hu. | 2. Le mois prochain c'est novembre. | 3. Il arrive en mars. |
|---|---|---|---|
| | 4. Le concert est la semaine prochaine. | 5. Le samedi, nous allons au parc. | 6. Demain c'est dimanche. |

| C | 1. C'est l'automne | 2. C'est l'été. | 3. C'est l'hiver. | 4. C'est le printemps. |
|---|---|---|---|---|

### 13.3 Frequency

| | |
|---|---|
| A | 1. Parfois, je mange un bol de fraises. \| 2. Ils vont souvent au parc. \| 3. Est-ce l'hiver ? \| 4. Je veux une tasse de chocolat chaud! \| 5. Elle arrive en août. En été, nous jouons aux échecs tous les jours. \| 6. C'est le soir ! La fête est à dix-neuf heures. \| 7. Chaque matin, nous prenons un gros petit-déjeuner ensemble. |
| B | 1. Each Sunday, he goes to the bakery and he eats a croissant. <br> 2. Each summer, we go to the beach. It's hot in August! <br> 3. It's April. In spring, I like to read in the garden. <br> 4. In winter, you wear an elegant black coat. You look beautiful! <br> 5. It's noon and I'm thirsty. Every afternoon, I drink a big glass of water. <br> 6. Each night, they watch TV together in the living room. |

## CHAPTER 14
### 14.1 Parler

| A | 1. Je parle français. | 2. Tu parles italien. | 3. Vous parlez espagnol. | 4. Nous parlons chinois. |
|---|---|---|---|---|
| | 5. Elle parle japonais. | 6. Il parle anglais. | 7. Ils parlent allemand. | 8. Elles parlent portugais. |

| B | 1. Nous parlons ensemble chaque semaine. \| 2. Ils se parlent une fois par mois. \| 3. Elles parlent parfois espagnol. \| 4. L'homme intelligent parle très bien le français. \| 5. Chaque matin, tu parles au bébé. \| 6. Je ne parle pas espagnol. \| 7. Elle parle beaucoup. \| 8. Pourquoi parles-tu à la vache ? |
|---|---|
| C | 1. I like to talk to my grandmother. She's very funny and interesting. <br> 2. I talk to Jane every week because we are good friends. <br> 3. Why do you talk to the cat? The cat doesn't speak English! <br> 4. Who is talking? Is it Emma and Esther? They talk too much. <br> 5. He talks to the dogs because he likes animals. |

### 14.2 Conjunctions

| A | 1. et | 2. ou | 3. mais | 4. ou | 5. mais | 6. et |
|---|---|---|---|---|---|---|
| B | 1. puis | 2. comme | 3. alors | 4. si | 5. comme | |

Speak Abroad
Academy

### 14.3 Prepositions

| A | 1. Après | 2. jusqu'à | 3. sans | 4. sauf | 5. avant | 6. pendant |
|---|---|---|---|---|---|---|
| B | 1. I go to school every day except Sunday. \| 2. He plays football until noon. \| 3. You are eating and drinking during an important concert. \| 4. They go to the museum with an old woman. \| 5. We don't like to eat before doing sports. ||||||
| C | 1. Nous mangeons le dessert après le dîner. \| 2. Je fais un gâteau sans sucre. \| 3. Ils parlent pendant le film. \| 4. Elle aime lire avant le petit-déjeuner. \| 5. Il boit du vin avec un homme intéressant. ||||||
| D | 1 \| 2 \| 5 \| 7 ||||||
| E | 1. Ils mangent le dîner après le déjeuner. \| 2. Je sors avec ma sœur. \| 3. Il va à l'école sans moi. \| 4. Elle mange avec moi. ||||||

## CHAPTER 15
### 15.1 Possessive Adjectives

| A | 1. Son livre \| 2. Mon chien \| 3. Notre voiture noire \| 4. Ton bureau \| 5. Son verre de vin \| 6. Leur belle vache \| 7. Votre fille intelligente |
|---|---|
| B | 1. Leur père est mon médecin. \| 2. Sa veste est rouge et ma veste est blanche. \| 3. Il ne parle pas à sa mère. \| 4. Leur maison est plus grande que notre maison. \| 5. Votre fils joue au football avec notre fils. \| 6. Ma sœur aime manger dans votre restaurant. |
| C | 1. Tes tomates. \| 2. Mes fleurs. \| 3. Ses manteaux. \| 4. Ses bières. \| 5. Leurs voitures. \| 6. Nos fromages. \| 7. Vos canapés. |
| D | 1. Ma sœur n'aime pas ta sœur. \| 2. Sa vache mange mes fleurs. \| 3. Où sont tes frères ? \| 4. Tes chats sont dans mon jardin. \| 5. La femme intelligente est leur avocat. \| 6. Nos voitures sont trop grandes pour tes/vos garages. \| 7. Parfois, nos filles vont au parc ensemble. |

### 15.2 Reflexive Pronouns & Verbs

| A | 1. Je m' | 2. Elle se | 3. Il se | 4. Nous nous | 5. Elles se | 6. Tu te | 7. Vous vous | 8. Ils se |
|---|---|---|---|---|---|---|---|---|
| B | 1. À huit heures | 2. Un quart d'heure || 3. Paul se brosse les dents | | 4. Il se rase | 5. Il s'habille ||
| C | 1. Il se déshabille. | 2. Je me prépare. || 3. Elles se regardent. || 4. Ils se rasent. |||
|  | 5. Tu te calmes. | 6. Nous nous réveillons. || 7. Elle s'habille. || 8. Vous vous reposez. |||

### 15.3 Pouvoir

| A | 1. Tu peux | 2. Je peux | 3. Elles peuvent | 4. Ils peuvent |
|---|---|---|---|---|
|  | 5. Vous pouvez | 6. Nous pouvons | 7. Elle peut | 8. Il peut |
| B | 1. Je ne peux pas aller au musée. 2. Tu ne peux pas manger de fromage. 3. Elle ne peut pas prendre le croissant. 4. Il ne peut pas parler à la vache. | 5. Vous ne pouvez pas préparer le petit-déjeuner. 6. Nous ne pouvons pas manger dans le jardin. 7. Ils ne peuvent pas parler français. 8. Ils ne peuvent pas porter de chaussettes à la plage. |||
| C | 1. C'est dimanche aujourd'hui. Il y a deux hommes devant ma maison. Ce sont mes amis. Nous allons au musée ensemble. \| 2. À 17 heures, je me prépare pour la fête. Je porte une belle robe noire et des chaussures blanches. \| 3. Pour le dessert ce soir, nous avons du gâteau. Veux-tu de la glace sur le gâteau ? \| 4. Ils sont une gentille famille. Ils ont trois filles intelligentes et une belle maison, mais je n'aime pas leur chien. \| 5. Mon frère aime la poésie et ma sœur le tennis. Et moi ? J'aime notre chat. \| 6. Au printemps, ils vont au parc. En été, ils vont à la plage. Il fait trop chaud, alors je vais à l'église. ||||